Britain In The 1970s

Michael Hodges

B.T. Batsford Ltd London

CONTENTS

© Michael Hodges 1989
First published 1989

Typeset by Tek-Art Ltd, West Wickham, Kent
Printed and bound in Great Britain by
Courier International Ltd, Tiptree, Essex
for the publishers
B.T. Batsford Ltd
4 Fitzhardinge Street
London W1H 0AH

ISBN 0 7134 5913 1

Note on Sources
Unless the source is specified, the quotations in the biographies of Paul Foot, Jeremy Seabrook, Peter Bush and the Maunsells are recorded conversations; and with Jack Jones and Barbara Castle the quotations come from letters to the writer.

Acknowledgments
The Author and Publishers would like to thank the following for their kind permission to reproduce illustrations: The Camera Press for figures 25, 26, 27 and 33; The Keystone Collection for figures 1, 3, 4, 7, 8, 12, 13, 14, 15, 16, 18, 20, 21, 22, 23, 24, 28, 29, 30, 31, 32, 34, 35, 36, 37, 41, 42, 44, 45, 50 and frontispiece; The Press Association for figure 19. Figures 11, 46, 47 and 48 are from the collection of the Author and figures 38, 40 and 43 from the collection of the Publisher.

Cover Illustrations
The colour photograph shows a panorama of North Sea oil platforms (courtesy Robert Harding Picture Library); the bottom left photograph shows the aftermath of the 1973 Old Bailey bomb explosion (courtesy The Keystone Collection); the bottom right photograph shows Ted Heath victorious in the 1970 General Election (courtesy The Keystone Collection).

THE 1970s

In his penetrating book, *The Seventies*, Christopher Booker (see pages 33-36) claims that this was, "arguably the most important decade in the twentieth century". There is some truth in Booker's statement, though few may have perceived it at the time. Gradually, it dawned on people that much of the wild optimism for mankind's future was misplaced, and the heady promises made by scientists, professionals, planners and technocrats of the sixties were illusory.

Politically, neither the Conservatives under Edward Heath (pages 13-16) nor Labour (Barbara Castle, pages 20-23) could grapple with the economic difficulties which were complicated by the energy crisis (1973 on) and relations with the trade unions (Jack Jones, pages 17-20). As government after government faltered, people seriously doubted Britain's will to be governed. "The ungovernability of Britain" was a cry that echoed down the seventies.

The emergence of Mrs Thatcher as Conservative Prime Minister (1979) provided to some a necessary order, "the return to the old values, the home-coming for traditional virtues, or (to others) reaction, the imposition of the barbarities of a system which the victors of 1945 had vowed would never again be tolerated" (Jeremy Seabrook, pages 40-43).

Minimum not maximum material expectations became the order of the day, be these expectations wage settlements, public expenditure or level of government borrowing. Mrs Thatcher's emphasis on self-denial and the primacy of the individual, her contempt for huge bureaucracies and trade union power, which stifled initiative and drained profits, impressed some people. Moreover, her puritanical manner may have reflected people's distaste for incidences of corruption in public life. Reginald Maudling, a Conservative minister, was involved with the corrupt building transactions of John Poulson; then there was the affair of the Liberal leader, Jeremy Thorpe, who was accused of conspiring to murder a homosexual friend. One of Harold Wilson's personal recommendations for the Honours List, Lord Kagan, was later imprisoned for fraud. Above all, perhaps, voting for Mrs Thatcher was Britain's reaffirmation in the law of Parliament after a decade of political instability when, at times, parliamentary democracy did seem vulnerable. Sub-consciously, this factor may have been more important to voters than their whole-hearted belief in Mrs Thatcher's radical-right philosophy.

High among sixties folk-heroes were architects like Sir Denys Lasdun and town planners. Their vision of regenerating inner cities led to soul-less housing estates marked by huge tower blocks which destroyed any sense of community, and created social distress and crime which none, apparently, had predicted. Examples include the North Peckham estates in South London which, "The council officially refers to as 'no-go areas,' and recommends "special safety procedures" for all workers going there.

1 Any doctor or teacher involved with high-rise tenants is familiar with the tension and aggression which they can sometimes experience.

There are no such procedures for residents. . . According to the residents the architect committed suicide. "He couldn't live with it," one of them said; "he couldn't live with what he'd done. But what about me? I have to!" (Joanna Coles: *The Spectator*). By the mid-seventies these misguided concepts of urban planning had been abandoned.

In technology, too, people questioned many assumptions. There were successes like Clive Sinclair's (pages 26-29) innovation in computer technology. Many technological advances did reach more homes. "Nine out of ten households had their own TV, refrigerator and vacuum cleaner. Three-quarters had a telephone. Many had a deep-freeze. Some form of central heating was the norm in any house built within the last 20 years." (Philip Ziegler's *Elizabeth's Britain*).

The oil crisis imposed many constraints on Britain, though some could be turned to advantage. Cars were designed to get more mileage per gallon. Too often there were expensive failures. The public were fascinated by the first supersonic airliner, Concorde, designed and produced by Anglo-French partnership. Passengers could now travel faster than a rifle bullet "without spilling their drink". But Concorde was expensive to operate and the boom when it broke the sound barrier aroused sustained opposition from conservationists. No more were built after 1979. The truth was that most people preferred to travel more cheaply rather than more quickly.

4 Freddie Laker's Skytrain was the complete opposite of Concorde – low cost transport across the Atlantic for those in less of a hurry to get there.

New generations of military and civil projects were abandoned – from Black Arrow, to tracked Hovercraft; from the Channel Tunnel to London's third airport. Southwark Borough had one of the highest levels of homelessness in London and planned to build a £70 million new civic hall. This project became a national scandal and was abandoned. Shirley Williams declared (1971) that for scientists, the social scientists, as for local councillors, "the party was over". The same year "the OECD (Organization for Economic Co-operation and Development) described in its report *Science, Growth and Society* how all Western governments had changed their minds about the benefits of science" (Anthony Sampson in *The Changing Anatomy of Britain*).

In 1978 Louise Brown became the world's first "test-tube" baby. While this miraculous scientific achievement brought new hope to childless couples, disquiet was aroused because this kind of medical practice might lead to eventual "cloning" of human beings.

2 This cartoon presents Concorde as a threat to the environment. The USA refused landing rights to the supersonic plane for a year. Other countries would not allow it to cross their airspace.

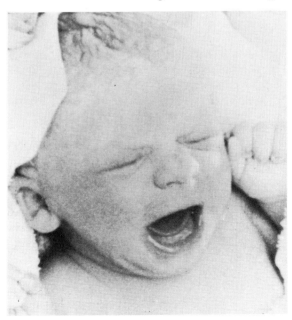

3 Louise Brown – the world's first test-tube baby.

Scientists knew about cloning frogs, and it was tempting to manipulate human tissues in a similar way. In Ira Levin's fantasy novel *The Boys from Brazil*, tissues from Hitler's body were implanted in women around the world, and a generation of Hitlers was created. Most scientists agreed to turn away from experiments with such macabre implications.

In medical science it was easy to feel that doctors were more concerned with sophisticated problem-solving operations such as "transplants" than with more traditional healing and comforting. Transplant surgery was only possible by advances in immunology. One of the most eminent immunologists was Peter Medawar who, in partnership with his wife, emerged "as the science-philosopher of the times". Significantly, Medawar stated, "Most of the problems that beset mankind call for political, moral and administrative rather than scientific solutions". One outstanding success was the development of the body scanner by Dr Geoffrey Hounsfield, which won him the Nobel Prize (1979).

The most politically sensitive of the sciences was nuclear physics. "After the world energy crisis the possibility of harnessing nuclear energy was more tantalizing than ever", (Anthony Sampson). But ordinary people as well as conservationists and ecologists were challenging the "bargain" by which governments could buy energy at the cost of their people's safety. The anti-nuclear lobby was greatly encouraged when the eminent nuclear physicist Sir Brian Flowers reported in 1976 to the government, "the dangers of building (nuclear) power stations had not been properly disclosed, and that the problems of dispersing nuclear fuel were still unresolved".

Flowers' report scandalized his scientific colleagues. However, his words were given an eerie ring of truth when the nuclear reactor at Three-Mile Island in America developed a serious radiation leak causing, "the most alarming accident in the history of civil and nuclear power". By 1979 some incoming Conservative politicians, who were torn between the self-interested claims of the nuclear, coal, oil and electrical power lobbies,

wondered, "Perhaps Tony Benn was right after all, perhaps only the people can decide" (A. Sampson).

There were few more contentious issues than the nuclear arms race. The argument shifted during the seventies. People urged that some of the resources for nuclear weapons should be directed to more humanitarian purposes. What was the point, people argued, of possessing a nuclear capacity to liquidate the world 20 times over, when once or twice could do the job. In his book, *The Arms Race*, Richard Headicar raises some disconcerting issues, "military expenditure comes very close to a million dollars a minute. . . One-quarter of the world's scientists are engaged on Research and Development of a military nature. . . The Third World nations spend more on arms than they receive in development aid." In a wider context Headicar observes, "For as long as there exists an unfair distribution of the wealth of the world and a misuse of its abundant resources, oppression and exploitation will continue."

The belief that people were becoming more alert to the limitations and misdirections of scientific applications was reassuring. Rarely was the scientific contradiction more strikingly exposed than when America landed two men on the moon (1969) with little benefit

"Must we? They're already in danger of becoming extinct."

5 The presence of North Sea oil off Scotland and disenchantment with central government intensified Scottish nationalism. By 1974 the Scottish Nationalists were close to being the largest party in Scotland – but a referendum in 1979 failed to achieve enough support in Scotland and Wales for devolution.

6 This cartoon implies that mankind will destroy itself unless it treats the environment with greater care.

7 The "Troubles" in Northern Ireland were never far from the news in the seventies. Six people were killed in these riots following the introduction of internment (imprisonment without trial) in 1972.

for mankind as a whole. Yet America seemed incapable of coping with problems on her own planet. Racism and violence in her own society were never far from the surface, and her inability to pacify or to arbitrate in the world's trouble spots was noticed by many Britons.

Racial disaffection had been smouldering in Britain throughout the seventies and presented a formidable social challenge. National Front provocation on the streets and disturbances at the Notting Hill carnival in London (1976) alerted people to potential trouble. That year Mark Bonham Carter, Chairman of the Community Relations Commission, warned, "The Black population are British, and they take the phrase equality of opportunity for what it means. I have no doubt we have not kept pace with the expectations of British-born Blacks." The 1976 Race Relations Act declared all forms of discrimination illegal. A commission for Racial Equality with powers of enforcing the Act was set up. Some people argued that no law on earth could change attitudes. There was talk of a backlash from disaffected and deprived whites who themselves might feel discriminated against.

In his play *Class Enemy* (1978), Nigel Williams provides insight into inadequate whites who feel threatened by blacks. One of the characters, Nipper, rants against immigrants:

. . . When they (blacks) get ter London vey go schraight ter the Foreign Office ter see their black mates an' their black mates fix 'em up wiv places on the black market — iss called that on account iss run by blacks. Oh, they pay a lot for the 'ouses. Forty thousand quid for a two room

7

8 The popularity of the natural health care and food products reflected public wariness of modern medical practices. The "thalidomide babies" – seriously handicapped by their mothers' use of this drug in the 1960s – reached adulthood in the seventies. Maxine Paine was the first of the 411 thalidomide children to start a full-time job – as sales assistant in a Do-it-Yourself shop.

flat in Wandsworf which is why all us bin on the waitin' list ten years . . . an whites lose their jobs but there ain't nuffink they can do on account of ver Labour Government's bin took over by vese blacks. . . .

Clearly the Nippers of this world need help.

They rail against blacks because they feel alienated from all society. Blacks happen to be a convenient and accessible target.

Feminism received a powerful impetus in 1970 when Germaine Greer published her book *The Female Eunuch*. Her view of suppressed woman existing in slavish submission to man was by no means novel. However, her book, "of high literary quality and deep scholarship which made some disturbing points" (Arthur Marwick in *British Society since 1945*), made an impact on many

9 Germaine Greer's *The Female Eunuch* was first published in paperback in 1971, and became one of the most influential books of the seventies.

women – and men. Magazines, such as the British *Cosmopolitan* and *Spare Rib*, both founded in 1972 were among the leaders in raising the controversial issues of abortion, rape, contraception and nuclear power. The Sex Discrimination Act (1975) was positive recognition of women's equal rights on pay, employment, education and provision of housing and services.

There was a strong resurgence of women's literature. Arthur Marwick suggests "If, when it is possible, to identify social and creative trends in writing, one such trend stressed the women's viewpoint." These reflections are seen in Beryl Bainbridge's *Sweet William* (1975) and Fay Weldon's *Praxa* (1978) – though Fay Weldon took the conventional line that the nature of woman was incompatible

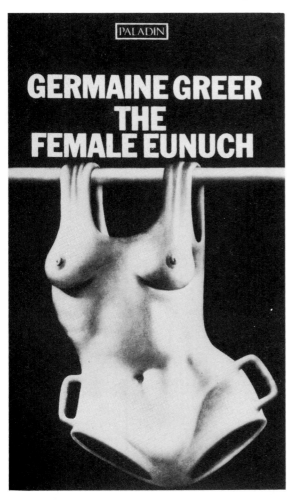

with feminist extremism.

Possibly films were replacing fiction as a reflection of contemporary issues. Alongside sensational fantasies like *The Exorcist*, *Jaws* and *Star Wars*, there were some outstanding films which struck at the roots of social tension. *A Clockwork Orange* depicted society's revenge on the violence of youth. *One Flew Over the Cuckoo's Nest* showed the mindless behaviour of psychiatric staff towards the mentally sick. Michael Tippett's (pages 50-52) opera, *The Ice Break*, was a powerful creation in an unexpected art-form. By the mid-seventies Pop art and fashion had reached the "ultimate frontiers" of innovation. The Punk and New Wave, along with reggae and disco music, pulled pop music back to its roots as music to dance to. People's tastes became more nostalgic. Shows like *The Boy Friend* revived the 1920s and *Grease* the 1950s, the latter starring the cult figure John Travolta. The guitarist John Williams and the composer Andrew Lloyd Webber tried to link classical with popular music. In this genre Lloyd Webber's musical *Evita* was a great success. In 1979 the most successful songwriter was Paul McCartney. He had broken away from his past with the Beatles and formed his own group Wings.

A symptom of a quieter mood was the upsurge of interest in the arts. "The concert halls were still full, the theatres busy. The queues outside the art galleries longer than ever – not so much in honour of the masterpieces of our own time, as because the appetite for the music, the plays and art works of the past had never been greater" (*The Seventies*).

British football performance was disappointing after England's 1966 World Cup success. Football managers seemed unable to cultivate the few players of rare promise. They preferred to suppress the exciting talents of such players as Hudson, Osgood and Trevor Francis for the sake of work-rate, robustness and mediocrity. This attitude might have been changed if Gerry Francis (Queen's Park Rangers), the heir to England's captaincy and a player of genius, had not been crippled.

Though the total number of serious crimes declined, violence and vandalism committed by young people increased. "Our traditional national values of tolerance and humour deteriorated, while football hooliganism, crime and political extremism increased." (Senior Civil Servant) To some extent these characteristics may have been protests by youth against the ineptitude and remoteness of leadership at all levels. On the other hand, "People may have increasingly searched for fulfilment in ways other than that of a rising standard of living, precisely because that living standard was not on offer . . ." (Senior Civil Servant).

Perhaps the extraordinary success of Richard Adams' allegorical novel, *Watership Down* (enjoyed by adult and child alike), provides an enduring reflection of the 1970s – of people acknowledging the consequences of their own wanton actions; and their quest to return to simpler values. Moreover, the story is a longing for a society which provides security without repression, and a world fit for children to grow up in joy and for the old to die in dignity.

10 The use of drugs in sport caused controversy throughout the decade. A Scottish footballer was sent home from the 1978 World Cup in Argentina for using "illegal stimulants". Generally, the law was more moderate – first offenders were fined, not imprisoned.

"I've had that you fool – where's the baton?"

11 A Welsh Border farm. The farmer who owns these sheep is a first generation farm owner. Many dreamed of leaving seventies city tensions behind for a more simple, rural way of life. But the cost of even repairing the roof of a farm such as this in 1970 would have bought the same property 20 years earlier.

POLITICIANS

The sixties were difficult years for the Conservative Party. Harold Macmillan, the one-time charismatic leader, had lost his magic. The leadership was controlled by inheritance, privilege and the Old Etonian network. Two General Elections were lost, and the Conservatives seemed to lose their way when they elected Sir Alec Douglas-Home (Fourteenth Earl of Home) successor to Macmillan as Prime Minister in 1963. Though an enlightened Scottish Border landowner, Home was scarcely equipped to lead a modern political party. Moreover, Harold Wilson, the opposition Labour leader, possessed an effective TV presence and a "technocratic command" which seemed more in line with contemporary Britain.

Douglas-Home's election caused much resentment from his colleagues. Ian Macleod and Enoch Powell resigned, while Lord Hailsham and R.A. Butler stayed on, affronted and embittered. When the Conservatives lost the 1964 General Election they turned to Edward Heath as their answer to Wilson. Heath's election as Tory leader was a classic case of the resilience of the Tory Party to adjust quickly and ruthlessly to the pressures and mood of a given time in history.

The cooperation of the trade unions was crucial to government social and economic policy. The key trade union leader was Jack Jones of the Transport and General Workers Union. By 1974 Heath felt his authority so undermined by the miners' strike that he called a General Election. He almost won, gaining more votes than Labour but five seats less. The bitterness of losing on a technicality rankled with him for years.

When the Winter of Discontent (1978-79) virtually brought the public services to a halt, none was more stunned or confused than

12 Ted Heath — victorious in the 1970 General Election.

James Callaghan's Labour government (1976-79). Barbara Castle was a forceful Labour politician and cabinet minister in Wilson's government. Her political diaries provide perceptive and honest insights into the harrowing political front of the middle seventies.

13 The Queen during the 1977 Silver Jubilee. The Duke of Edinburgh had said earlier that year: "If people feel it [the monarchy] has no part to play, then for goodness sake let's end the thing on amicable terms." But the monarchy seemed to play as big a part in British life in the seventies as ever before.

Writing on the walls.
Gossip everywhere.
One O'Clock Gun, have you heard
    about that?
They've driven the old man out.
Smashing windows, you vandals.
Terrible, isn't it, it's damn terrible.
My kid fell on the playground the
    other day.
Mums complaining.
Bonfire night's the worst.
They come round pinching your fences.

Tommy just got stuck in Ford Towers lifts.
Now it's night time. Everyone in bed.

Vandals come out, smashing windows.
I heard they battered an old lady up
    and took her bread.
It's terrible.

Joanne Edwards, aged 12, won the Poetry Society national "Children as Poets" award (1979/80) with this poem on growing up in a high-rise in Birkenhead.

Edward Heath (1916-   )

Edward Heath was born in Broadstairs. His family provides an interesting example of social mobility (advancement) over several generations. His great-grandfather was a merchant seaman. Heath's father, Will, was a carpenter before buying up his employer's building firm. His mother had been in "service" to a Hampstead family and she brought middle-class manners into the Heath home. "With her looks she could have done better!" commented Heath's maternal grandmother on her daughter's engagement to Will Heath.

From Ramsgate Grammar School, Edward Heath went to Balliol College, Oxford. During the Second World War he became a Lieutenant Colonel in the Honourable Artillery Company and he entered Parliament in 1950. "That intake in the Commons," wrote Andrew Roth, the biographer, "was exceptional in the large proportion of its new Tory entrants who were ex-officers – and who were professionally competent and had made their way without benefit of family wealth and connections."

"Ted Heath had his own paternalist tendencies", wrote Anthony Sampson in *The Changing Anatomy of Britain*,

but after he led his party to a second defeat in 1966 he was more determined to sharpen his attack on socialism. He played down his old liberal sympathies for welfare, the unemployed or the Third World, and advocated a much more self-interested and commercialized nation. . . His domestic slogan was "stand on your own feet" . . . and he put together policies to make industry more competitive and government leaner and more efficient.

In 1970 Wilson dissolved Parliament and called a General Election. Traditional Tories were disheartened by Heath's bleak crusade, projected in rather a wooden, though sincere, style, and many people were very surprised when, against the odds, he won the Election with a majority of 30. But national disquiet had been mounting at increasing trade union unrest and the feeling that Labour was pandering to them. Another contributing factor was, perhaps, the austere economic policies of Labour's Chancellor, Roy Jenkins, who had sought to get the economy under control through constraints on public spending.

For a year things went relatively well. Heath had promised his supporters "a change so radical, a revolution so quiet and yet so total that it will go beyond the programme for a parliament," and he rejected consensus:

There never was a consensus in the sense of a deliberate effort of will. The parties never came together in their policies.

Warnings that industrial organizations were finding it difficult to "stand on their own feet" came when Upper Clyde Shipbuilders and Rolls Royce, the showpiece of British engineering and craftsmanship, went bankrupt (1971), though the Government did rescue the aerospace division. 1972 marked the watershed year when Heath seemed to lose direction. Britain was finding it difficult to sell her products, often out-dated and over-priced, in competitive world markets. The outdated attitude that "the world owes Britain a living" was dying hard. On top of this prices were rising continuously, which meant that money was losing its value (inflation). Heath's relations with the trade unions were always tense. When he tried to curb the power of the unions with his Industrial Relations Act (1971), hostility mounted. Philip Ziegler wrote in *Elizabeth's Britain:* "The unions believed that the new act would make it more difficult for them to look after their members; they resolved to defy it to the limits of the law, and if necessary beyond".

Sometimes it looked as if the Law itself

allowed "illegal" opposition when, for instance, an obscure person called the Official Solicitor (a position hitherto "believed extinct") stepped in to secure the release from prison of five dockers who had defied the Industrial Relations Act. Already one and a half million engineers had gone on strike in protest at the Act. Indeed by 1974 employers, as well as the unions, were denouncing the Act and ignoring it.

The first serious challenge to Heath's authority came when the coal miners went on strike in 1972, after an overtime ban. The strike was brilliantly organized by a hitherto unknown figure from Barnsley called Arthur Scargill. Scargill left little doubt that the strike was political: "We had to declare war on them [the Conservatives], attack the vulnerable points." And when Scargill's flying pickets, a new force in strike-strategy, forced the police to evacuate and close down the Birmingham

14 Ted Heath campaigning with Margaret Thatcher and Lord Carrington, in the second of the 1974 General Elections. Heath's premiership had been ended by the crisis election earlier that year.

Coke Depot, Scargill asserted with some truth that "The working class had only to flex its muscles and it could bring government, employers, society, to a total standstill." Two years later

he claimed some credit for forcing Ted Heath to declare an election, thus causing his downfall. (*The Changing Anatomy of Britain*)

When Heath conceded the miner's claim he had renounced his principles of no consensus and a "tougher, leaner Britain standing on its own feet." By 1972 Heath was convinced that government had to intervene to revive industry and that an Incomes policy could stem the tide of inflation. In his historic "U-turn" he passed the new Industry Act which provided large funds to the Department of Trade and Industry.

Other measures included, first, a wage "freeze" and then statutory levels of prices, pay, rent and dividend increases. People tended to criticize Heath for such fundamental policy inconsistencies, but as Prime Minister he had been appalled at the deceptive boom in property and financial speculations while industry, the creator of wealth, foundered. Nor would Heath agree to causing still higher unemployment as a means of controlling the unions. Many charged Heath with weakness which would store up more trouble in the future. Perhaps Heath's political advisor, Douglas Hurd, came near the truth: "No one of Mr Heath's background and generation could easily dismiss rising unemployment (2.6 per cent in 1970, 3.8 per cent in 1972) as unimportant."

Heath's difficulties were compounded by the oil crisis (1973). Following the Israeli-Arab War that year, oil supplies to Britain and other western countries were first drastically reduced and, soon after, the price quadrupled. A steady supply of oil at a stable price was crucial to economic stability. Overnight, manufacturing costs soared.

These costs were reflected in prices. The price of petrol shot up from 30p a gallon to around £1.20. One consequence was that Britain spent far more on imports than before. From 1971-75 Britain's balance of payments (trading position with the world) was the worst in history, a debt to other countries of £1044 million. Yet Britain persisted in expensive "fantasy" projects like Concorde financed by "fantasy money" (page 35). One of the biggest spenders was cabinet member Keith Joseph, who spent huge sums on reorganizing the National Health Service. Unemployment did fall but inflation remorselessly rose.

Another consequence was people's determination to keep up their standard of living. The result was a vicious circle of workers pressing for wage claims to keep up with ever-increasing shop and services prices.

16 A moment of triumph for Egyptian soldiers in the 1973 Middle East War. The war led directly to oil price rises and the energy crisis of 1973-74.

17 Western industrial nations resented the large oil price rises of 1973, but oil producers were reflecting the market value of their commodity.

Industrial unrest now came to a head. The oil scarcity enhanced the importance of the mining industry. In November 1973 (the time of year when coal demand becomes heavy) the miners pay negotiations broke down and they started an overtime ban. They were supported by the railmen and power workers. Heath was beleaguered. By Christmas he had imposed a three-day working week to conserve fuel – though cynics said Britain had worked on that basis for years! In February 1974, 81 per cent of the miners voted for an all-out strike as Heath rejected their pay claim. Heath called a General Election with the appeal, "Who governs Britain?" – with the implication that if he lost then constitutional government would be the loser.

Heath narrowly lost. Many people believed that the daunting times required a different leader.

Heath's greatest historic achievement was to bring Britain into the European Economic Community (EEC). He was always a European and his sustained resolution crowned nearly 15 years of negotiations. But even this success seemed flawed. The timing was wrong. "If you had come in 15 years earlier", said Robert Marjolin (one of the framers of the Treaty of Rome), "you would have got the benefit of the European boom, and your people would have accepted Europe."

In February 1975 Heath was replaced as leader of the Conservative Party by Margaret Thatcher. He retired to the back benches where he has remained largely an isolated and rather ineffective critic of his successor.

18 Some of the "oil money" came back to London in the form of real estate investment. The For Sale notice on this West End property is worded in Arabic as well as English – a sign of who the buyers were expected to be.

Jack Jones (1913-   )

Jack Jones was one of the outstanding British trade union leaders of his generation. Throughout most of the 1970s Jones was General-Secretary of the most powerful union, the Transport and General Workers (TGWU). The TGWU had nearly two million members, one-sixth of the trade union membership, and was the largest union in Europe. Commanding this kind of power-base, with its immense political potential, Jones was said to be "the second most powerful man in Britain".

Jones was brought up in the "hard school" of Liverpool poverty. He became a docker and before long "Socialism became Jack's religion", says his wife. He went to Spain in the 1930s to fight for the elected socialist government against the rebel General Franco, and was wounded in the shoulder.

Many people's attitude to Jack Jones was coloured by their resentment of trade unionists. They regarded trade union policy as an attempt to get the maximum and give the minimum, and this seemed one cause for Britain's lacklustre economic performance. One image of trade union power was the 1978-79 "Winter of Discontent". The public sector services were crippled by strikes, as groups of workers fought the government, and each other, for increased wages and the restoration of pay differentials. Hospitals refused to admit patients and a leader of the Health Services Workers (COHSE) warned on television, "If it means lives lost, that is how it must be." Many found such an attitude hard to forgive.

Harold Wilson (Prime Minister 1974-76) believed that Britain could only recover her prosperity with the cooperation of the unions.

Wilson was determined to conciliate the unions, promising them new privileges in return for supporting the Social Contract (see below) without exacting any serious promises for the unions to cooperate in wage restraint (*The Changing Anatomy of Britain*).

19 Jack Jones, General Secretary of the Transport and General Workers Union 1969-78.

Jack Jones's support was crucial as other unions tended to follow where he led.

There always was a need for trade unions to try to influence governments. . . The essence of the "Social Contract" represented an acceptance of the fact that the services and benefits, vital to civilized progress, and paid for collectively through Government, are part of the "social wage". In short, trade unionists accepted that pensions, the NHS, child benefits, good housing and decent schools are vital to their true level of income; that they must be paid for, and that allowances should be made for this provision by employers and trade unions in wage negotiations, price policies and industrial investment programmes.

This voluntary "Social Contract" was much maligned. People felt, rightly or wrongly, that the Labour Government had conceded exceptional power to the trade unionists. The historian from Sussex University, Keith Middlemas, wrote,

The terms represented the most complete capitulation by the Labour party to the industrial movement. (*Politics in Industrial Society*)

Within a year some of the Labour government regretted giving such responsibilities to one unelected group in society, albeit one strong in numbers and muscle. In 1974-5 disagreement mounted between government and trade unions as fuel, food and raw material costs rose, leading to higher inflation.

A policy of relating wage claims to the increases in the cost of living failed to achieve results fast enough. Some ministers, Denis Healey in particular, wanted wage restraint as a major objective – the trade union view was that wage restraint was not "the be all and end all", and there should be more emphasis on industrial investment and productivity in solving the economic problems. (Jack Jones)

Disillusionment followed quickly. "The only give and take in the contract", complained Joel Barnett, the Chief Secretary to the Treasury, "was that the government gave and the unions took." Even Barbara Castle was dismayed: "We have heaped goodies on the unions but they have delivered nothing in return." And Anthony Sampson wrote,

For a party so closely linked with the unions, the social contract was a staggering failure . . . many

in the cabinet began to despair of the unions' irresponsibility.

However, it was Jones's initiative which in 1975 brought some stability. To control excessive wage claims Jones suggested a £6 per week pay rise for everyone. Jones had always disliked a percentage pay system because,

it seemed unfair that low paid workers should receive less than higher paid people when it came to making compensation for increases in the cost of living.

The government seized on Jones's idea enthusiastically. But he needed to sell his pay formula to his union members, who were becoming impatient with wage limits. For a time "Jones held back his militants by the force of his rhetoric and personality".

For a year the voluntary policy succeeded. Inflation fell and the government was afforded breathing space. Nor did the public sector unions breach the policy. However, the wage policy was broken when the private company, Ford Motors, awarded a wage claim of 15 per cent.

In September 1976 the Trade Union Congress decided on an orderly return to normal collective bargaining, but placing stress on raising minimum wages and reduction in working hours . . . the government pressed for a continuation of a pay policy and insisted on a (small) percentage approach. The ensuing phase was a compromise and much less acceptable to the majority of workers. (Jack Jones)

In 1977 the miners put in for a 90 per cent pay rise; the railwaymen followed with a 63 per cent claim. This was just the beginning and the Winter of Discontent was still to come.

In 1976 Michael Charlton interviewed Jack Jones on television "We have to raise our eyes far and beyond wages and working

20 *The Times* suspended publication for the first time in its history, when management and union negotiations over the introduction of new technology broke down in December 1978.

conditions. . . We have to understand that we are working towards a better world", Jones said. Christopher Booker was sceptical of Jones's world:

Mr Jones has very little time for the English Parliamentary system. He admitted he would only be prepared to cooperate with a Conservative government so long as it pursued Socialist policies. But is Mr Jones a democrat at all? (*The Seventies*)

Seven years earlier Jones addressed the TGWU when he was elected General-Secretary: "We aim to make the TGWU the most democratic union in the world." While some viewed Jones with dread as an anti-democrat who almost single-handedly could topple governments, he spent nine years weakening the "dictatorial" style of his union leadership which, Ernest Bevin, the founder of the TGWU, had created in 1922.

Ironically, Jones became the victim of his own democratic ideas when his delegates ignored his advice and carried a motion for a return to "unfettered collective bargaining" (1977).

To my mind the acceptance of majority decisions is the essence of democracy. It is important to abide by the decision whilst trying to change it. (Jack Jones)

This conference was a momentous and historic occasion. Anthony Sampson recalls

Jones's lean and tense face confronted his bitter delegates, warning them that unleashing wages would generate a new wave of inflation and bring down the Labour government. He was met with heckling and boos, and the head of the union for the first time in its history was defeated by his own delegates.

Within a year Jack Jones had resigned, and soon afterwards Mrs Thatcher became Prime

Minister. To this day his fight for defenceless people goes on: Britain's pensioners are now the object of his undiminished passion and energy.

21 The "Winter of Discontent" in 1978-79 saw rubbish piling up as dustmen and many other groups of workers struck for higher pay. The Labour Government fell as a result – as Jack Jones had predicted.

Barbara Castle (1910-   )

Barbara Castle has been a passionate socialist all her life. At the age of six she wrote her first political speech on the back of an envelope: "More houses are needed". Barbara Castle was born in Bradford, and after attending Bradford Girls' Grammar School went to St Hugh's College, Oxford. Her father, a tax-inspector, inspired her commitment to public service which survives to this day. In 1937 Mrs Castle was elected to St Pancras Borough Council. She became Member of Parliament for Blackburn (1945) which she represented for 34 unbroken years.

In Harold Wilson's Labour government (1974-76) Barbara Castle was Secretary of State for the Social Services, and thus was at the centre of the mid-seventies cut-and-thrust of national affairs.

The 1970s were the battleground of ideas on how to manage the economy. Since the war there had been all-party agreement in the belief that government must shoulder the responsibility to see that the country's resources were fully employed, her people cared for and properly trained. Even Ted Heath accepted that responsibility in principle.

Belief in the trade union movement was an Article of Faith to Castle:

If there is an answer to this country's problems it lies in this inchoate [undeveloped] union between our government and the unions. I have always believed that our only hope is to make the unions more, not less political. . . Our job is to make them exercise positive power.

However, doubts on Labour/trade union collaboration were evident in the late sixties. Wilson was "privately wishing that the Labour Party could break away from the unions".

In spite of her faith in the unions she admitted deep concern about unofficial strikes.

The right of an employee to withdraw his labour is one of the essential freedoms of democracy. But I was deeply concerned lest abuse of the strike weapon should damage the trade union movement.

Her principle of making the unions more responsible and for reducing the number of unofficial "wildcat" strikes was stamped on her policy document *In Place of Strife* (1967). The document also provided the government with discretionary powers of intervention into industrial disputes. This scheme was dropped when it became clear that trade unions and some government ministers objected. Therefore, whatever sentiment may have still existed between the Labour party and their historic supporters, it was clear that the mood of the unions would not easily tolerate statutory restrictions on their rights.

22 Barbara Castle — a great reformer, who increased pensions and provided a new charter for the disabled. Castle secured the growth of the National Health Service, and introduced a Child benefit Scheme which gave the mother funds to spend on her children.

The basis of Harold Wilson's policy in 1974 was the Social Contract. The principle of the Social Contract was to bring peace to the factory floor without legal intervention. For a while this genuine attempt at reconciliation impressed the country. Wilson was confident enough to call a General Election in October 1974, when Labour increased its parliamentary majority over the Conservatives to 42, Labour holding a narrow majority of three over all the parties combined.

"The trade unions responded well to the new approach," wrote Castle. But this optimism did not endure. Within a year Barbara Castle was writing:

Joel Barnett [the Chief Secretary to the Treasury] has been to see Harold [Wilson], begging to be released from the Treasury. He wants out before the crash comes. The outlook for public expenditure programmes is bleak indeed. I spent the morning soldiering on to complete our draft of the social wage document, but I have a feeling it will never see the light of day. Things have gone too far for that.

Yet the unions go on cheerfully with their demands, as though none of this had anything to do with them. . . The TUC social service committee had unfolded a list of social policy items on which they wanted immediate action, such as increase in unemployment benefit, which will cost millions.

Typical of the constraint under which the economy operated at this time was the experience of British Steel. The chairman, Sir Monty Finniston, had announced 20,000 redundancies by closing old, high-cost steel plants in an effort to reduce the corporation's operating losses, then running at £2.5 million a week. Tony Benn, Secretary of State for Industry, resisted this decision tooth and nail

telling the unions he is going to insist on being the boss, and no redundancies. Tonight in the Lords, Watkinson has made a swingeing attack on him [Tony Benn], more or less threatening a strike of the whole of British Industry unless Harold gets rid of him. . . On every hand there is the feeling among our own people that the

23 Problems in the steel industry were nothing new. In January 1973 over two thousand steelworkers from North Wales clashed with police outside the House of Commons after marching to Westminster to protest against the closure of the Shotton plant.

economy is out of control: a mood which is fed by Harold's absence. . . (Castle Diaries)

Clearly the Social Contract was not working. Whatever the government spent was never enough and could not be afforded without building up massive debts to confront future generations. In 1976 the world bankers, the International Monetary Fund (IMF), stepped in and refused to lend Britain any more money unless the government drastically cut back on public expenditure. Apart from the humiliation of an outside banker determining Britain's internal policies, the IMF intervention shattered the socialist aspirations of the Labour government and, some said, "broke the heart of the Labour Party".

In spite of the daunting problems and, in the end, the failure of Wilson's government to stimulate the economy, Barbara Castle's department had some striking success in relieving social distress (see fig. 22).

Barbara Castle held firm and positive views outside the political arena, not least regarding the position in society of women. To Castle, women's rights were based on "patriotism", in the sense that unless the talent and energy of women are released then a vital national resource is being wasted to the detriment of the nation's wealth and creativeness. The International Women's Year (1975) and the Sex Discrimination Act (1975) were important milestones in the wider emancipation of women, to which causes Castle provided a thrust. When Margaret Thatcher was elected leader of the Conservative Party (1975) Castle wrote

I can't help feeling a thrill. . . After all, men have been running the show as long as anyone can remember and they don't seem to have made much of a job of it. I think it will be a good thing for the Labour Party too. There's a male

dominated party for you – not least because the trade unions are male-dominated, even the ones that cater for women.

"The 1970s", she wrote,

were a watershed in economic policy. Government by consent gave way to government by brute economic force, of which unemployment was the major instrument. . . The Social Contract had been a conscious attempt to involve workers in the decisions which affected their lives. It was now dismissed as irrelevant.

The famous Marxist historian, E.J. Hobsbaum, struck the root of the contradictory position of the Labour Party:

How could they reconcile equality with efficiency, industrial democracy with capitalist control, nationalization of the media with freedom of speech, protection of British industry with support for the Third World? (from "The Forward March of Labour Halted?", extracted from *The Changing Anatomy of Britain*).

Barbara Castle resigned from the cabinet when Jim Callaghan succeeded Wilson (1976), and from 1979-86 was an influential and highly respected Member of the European Parliament.

ENTREPRENEURS

Few industrial nations were as badly prepared as Britain to absorb, let alone overcome, the economic shocks of the oil crisis and the recession which bedevilled trading in the seventies. Commenting on Britain's faltering industrial performance, Professor Wiener of Texas observed "The world's first great industrial nation has never been comfortable with industrialization." The historian, Correlli Barnet, wrote in 1975

The Victorian public school is one of the keys to our decline, turning out by means of curriculum and the moulding influence of school life alike a governing class ignorant of, and antipathetic towards, sciences, technology and industry.

The successful businessman, Sir James Goldsmith, himself an Old Etonian, said, "Very few successful people in business have come out of the public schools mould".

Some companies aped the public schools ethos and operated along hierarchical military lines. The British Aluminium Company, for instance, seemed to prefer to recruit for their management trainee scheme ex-National Service officers from, ideally, the "Sacred Seven" schools, rather than chemists or metallurgists. The directors owned a yacht which they justified by experimenting with different paint reactions on its aluminium hull.

Overmanning was another deep-rooted practice which led to products priced at uncompetitive levels in order to pay for excess labour. A number of people, including Jack Jones, supported some form of industrial democracy. The Bullock Report (1977) recommended that

companies' boards should have an equal number of workers and shareholders representatives with all the workers directors chosen by the unions.

Management disliked the prospect of worker-directors nominated by their union with instructions, perhaps, to obstruct. Unionists, too, resisted the idea which would close the gap between management and trade unions. They were afraid the trade unions historic role might be irreversibly altered.

Investment in industry was another contention. Lord Lever, a former Labour minister, blamed many of Britain's economic ills on "the British failure to channel savings into investment."

As hostility mounted against strikes, trade union leaders retaliated by condemning capitalists for creating an "investment-strike" – i.e. a failure to invest in new machinery, training and techniques for the future. But when trade unions controlled their own pension fund investments, they were said to be

more capitalist than you or me; it's hard to restrain them from investing everything abroad (Trade Union Pension Fund Manager).

Richard Giordano, an American, was brought in to rescue the British Oxygen Company. He was astonished at

the lack of control of subsidiaries round the world, the demoralized state of the managers, the power of the unions and the widespread overmanning. He was baffled by the British class system but ignored it, not looking to Oxbridge for his managers. (*The Changing Anatomy of Britain*)

By the end of the seventies, leading firms such as Courtaulds, the textile giant, had shredded one-third of their employees. British Leyland collapsed spectacularly in 1973. The motor car industry had been a "protected species"; the prosperity of tens of thousands who supplied component parts depended on a

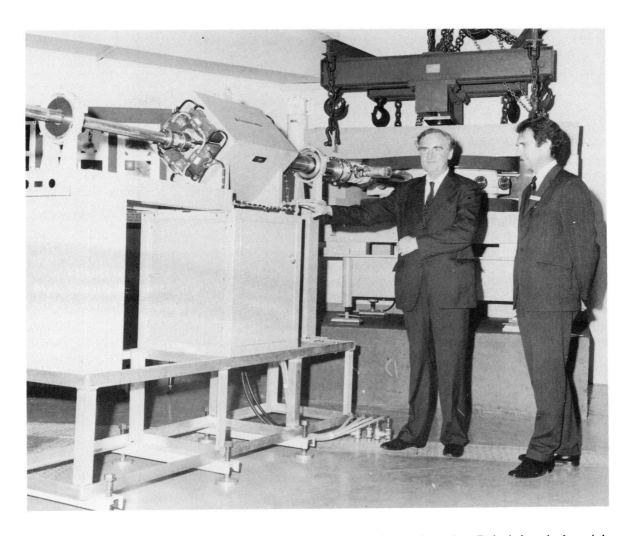

24 Sir Alan Cottrell, former Government Chief Scientific Adviser, believed that industrial applied science was being neglected in Britain in favour of pure research – "the less commercial the better".

buoyant car manufacturing performance. The government was very reluctant to let the car industry disintegrate. ICI (Imperial Chemical Industries) was a barometer for Britain's industrial performance with its brilliant scientific research, vast range of products and sales success since the 1930s. In the mid-seventies a British Rail manager boasted to an ICI man that BR was bigger. "Maybe", replied the ICI man, "but we've got more passengers". By 1979 one-fifth of ICI's manpower had become redundant.

Daunting though Britain's industrial problems were, several outstandingly successful businessmen pointed to new directions of trade. They included Giordano, who dramatically increased British Oxygen's profits in the middle of the recession, Michael Edwardes (a South African) who revived British Leyland, James Goldsmith, Clive Sinclair and, perhaps the most colourful of all, "Tiny" Rowland. These entrepreneurs were mostly "outsiders". Cosmopolitan by background and in outlook, they possessed a global vision of the business scene. Many possessed colourful personalities, a restless spirit and little respect for British finance houses and government regulations which obstructed their ambitions.

Clive Sinclair (1940-   )

Unlike many successful entrepreneurs of the 1970s, Clive Sinclair was born in London of English parents and was educated at English independent schools. However, Sinclair was always an "outsider"; he went to 13 different schools. His physics teacher recalls,

Sinclair was mad on radios. Physics then consisted of heat, light, sound and magnetism, but Clive couldn't be bothered with those things.

Sinclair left Highgage School early, and rejected university because he believed, "electrical engineering courses then available had little to offer me".

Sinclair is entirely self-taught in electronics. From his early years he was obsessed with inventing things. At 22 he borrowed £50 and set up his firm Sinclair Radionics, which sold repaired radios by mail order. He remembers "with pride" his first invention:

I thought there was a need for a small calculator and designed the whole thing from start to the actual production in nine months.

This famous pocket calculator, six inches (15.2 cm) long, was about 20 times smaller than the smallest one then available. By selling direct through mail order he did not have to raise the selling price to allow for the retailer's profit margin.

Difficulties, however, arose from the start and, up to a point, were a consequence of his success. Initially he was "overwhelmed with orders" (for the calculator) and his design won several international awards. But he had alerted his powerful competitors.

The Americans copied his design and undercut his prices, while the Japanese designed a new and better silicon chip. Sinclair suddenly found he "couldn't compete". His profits sank and the calculator was withdrawn. (Angela Levin in the *Observer*)

25 Clive Sinclair: "Doing for 10p what any fool can do for £1" made his products accessible to the mass market.

Setbacks never daunted Sinclair. Following quickly on top of his calculator came

the world's most radical digital watch which, since all the circuitry was a single chip, could be sold more cheaply than anything else on the market. Unfortunately his quality control wasn't good enough and whole case-loads were faulty.

By 1975, the pattern of Sinclair's operation was established: scientific vision combined with advanced technology applied to genuine market needs but flawed by poor quality-control which led to unsold stocks. These technical problems were made even worse by poor management. Sinclair lacked experience in running a company which had grown rapidly from 50 to 400 employees. Sinclair explained:

When small companies grow quickly, they need to reorganize quickly. I knew next to nothing about how to look after 400 people, about increased production and stock control. I was looking for a good manager to take over from me, but I didn't find one in time.

These setbacks led to a "mammoth cash crisis". To stay in business Sinclair reluctantly accepted £4.5 million investment of public funds from the National Enterprise Board. But he lost his independence at the same time. The partnership was uneasy. His controllers refused him money for research into his miniature flat screen television, which Sinclair called his "heart and soul".

26 The Sinclair ZX81: the first computer sold to the public for under £100.

When Sinclair left he was "determined to keep Sinclair Research (his new company) at a manageable size". He employed no more than 12 people in modest offices in Cambridge, delegated the production to outside firms and established very successful research links with Southampton and Exeter Universities.

In 1980 Sinclair launched perhaps his most imaginative product – the ZX81, the world's first computer selling at under £100; measuring only nine inches (22.9cm) by seven inches (17.8cm) and weighing 12 oz (340g). The computer was for the home. Once again hitches marred the product's success, and now the credibility of Sinclair himself. Hundreds of thousands of people waited months beyond Sinclair's promised deadline for computers they had already paid for. Even when the customers received their computer, "many had makeshift components and a large percentage failed to work properly". Complaints poured into the Office of Fair Trading. To avoid prosecution, Sinclair had to promise never to treat the public in the same way again.

The Advertising Standards Authority ordered computer magazines not to carry Sinclair advertisements which promised delivery in 28 days. "We take our lessons very much to heart", Sinclair assured people. But a recent brain-child, the electric car, proved quite unreliable. By 1986 Sinclair faced such debts and unsold stock that he was compelled to sell everything, including his company name to a rival company, Amstrad.

For an entrepreneur who was voted "Young Businessman of the Year" and knighted in 1983, Sinclair's business record might seem dubious. His critics dismiss him as "just an assembler". This seems to miss the point. An engineer, Jim Westward, who had been employed by Sinclair, said, "He has an inexhaustible supply of ideas. He works on the basis that all problems are surmountable. . . He is a man who finds it hard to say 'No' even when the problem cannot be overcome." The mechanics of assembling the product itself never really interested Sinclair.

Writing in *The Financial Times*, Alan Cave questions much of Sinclair's success, and some of his criticisms have been acknowledged by Sinclair himself. More disturbingly, Cave challenges Sinclair's reputation where he is believed most indestructible – his scientific creativeness. "It takes no great inventiveness", writes Cave to dream up gadgets like pocket calculators or TV sets. The science fiction writers have done it all before.

This rather glib observation is like saying Shakespeare wrote nothing original because words had been discovered long before.

Doubtless some of the praise of Sinclair may be excessive; he is "One of the most prodigious inventors since Leonardo da Vinci", according to *The Sunday Times*. But perhaps the truest reflection comes from a City backer:

Clive should spend his time inventing new

27 The Sinclair ZX81 in use, with TV set as monitor and cassette deck for software input.

products – an area where he is an undisputed genius – not running around controlling a business with £100m turnover and volatile profits.

Some might see Clive Sinclair as representative of a chronic problem of British industry – the inability to turn brilliant inventions into dependable products. Apart from technology and mathematics Sinclair is interested in poetry, music and the theatre. "Technology is a force for freedom" he has said, and looks forward to a time when "prisoners would roam free in society – monitored by signals emitted from electric headbands." He continues to explore the kind of scientific frontiers which the public regard with a mixture of fascination and nervousness.

"Tiny" Rowland (1917-   )

A "Revolutionary Capitalist" is how "Tiny" Rowland describes himself with some justification. Rowland was never intimidated by the conventions of doing business the British way, nor was he susceptible to British government policies. Rowland's great advantage was his rootlessness.

He belonged to no nation – born in India, half-German, half-English, beginning his career in Southern Rhodesia (now Zimbabwe). (*The Changing Anatomy of Britain*)

Consequently, Rowland traded easily with countries without the constraints of nationality or of allegiance to a particular political and trading tradition. His dealings in Africa were typical. In the immediate post-colonial years many businessmen detached their trading interests, where they could, from Central Africa. Not so Rowland. One of his rivals had said, "It can be easier to make money out of chaos than out of order, provided you know what you want." And Rowland knew.

He rushed round the newly-independent Black states, establishing close personal relationships with their leaders with his customary hospitality, acquiring concessions, trading rights, newspapers and even a railway in Malawi. (Anthony Sampson)

Of this last acquisition Rowland recalled,

Everyone said I was mad because railways never make money, but it enabled me to obtain other interests. (Conje and Ling in *Lonrho: Portrait of a Multinational*)

Rowland assisted several Black leaders in their domestic struggles for power. Few of them ever forgot his consistent support and favours. Remarkably, Rowland managed to maintain his ties with Black Africa and still prosper in White South Africa, where he controlled profitable interests in platinum mines and printing works. Only President Nyerere of Tanzania expelled his company in 1978 for "subverting the freedom struggle in southern Africa". But within a few years Rowland and Nyerere were reconciled.

Tiny Rowland began his career as a farmer in Southern Rhodesia. His first opportunity came when he was brought in to revive the moribund London and Rhodesian Mining and Land Company (Lonrho). The chairman was Angus Ogilvy, who later married Princess Alexandra, a cousin of the Queen. Before long

Rowland left the other directors panting behind him. . . He never discussed his management methods and shrouded most of his operations in secrecy. (*The Changing Anatomy of Britain*)

28 "Tiny" Rowland, on his way to the Law Courts during the battle with Sir Basil Smallpeice for the control of Lonrho.

Not for him the laborious business of reporting back to "absent" retired Whitehall directors and delaying action until corporate decisions had been reached.

A colleague has explained Rowland's success;

He was brought up against a background of restless danger, so his mind never worked in conventional ways. He looks for opportunities and deals where other people least expect them, and he makes use of his relationships with his famous persistence and charm.

Rowland's enterprises have ranged from building the Beira oil pipeline through Mozambique to land-locked Zimbabwe (1960s), to recent plans for re-opening the Benguela railway from Angola to the copper mines of central Africa.

Above all, Lonrho was successful. The group invested in high-risk, high-reward ventures in countries where other groups were afraid to go. Rowland was among the first to invest in Nigeria after the civil war, and Lonrho has recently invested 160 million dollars to modernize the Ashanti goldfields in Ghana. Half of Lonrho's profits come from his African interests.

It was in Britain that Rowland's trading methods annoyed the major business and government institutions. He even attracted the attention of the Department of Trade which spent 18 months investigating Lonrho's trading practices. Rowland's trading base in Britain began with Hadfields Steelworks, Whyte and Mackay Distillers, the Volkswagen agency and casinos.

He handled Britain rather like Africa. . . He never respected the formalities of the City of London. (Anthony Sampson)

Soon his maverick style of management caused a national furore:

Traditional British bankers and businessmen dreaded and distrusted him, but he flourished on their rejection and he showed an irresistible charisma to his own followers, as he led them on to new adventures, keeping one step ahead of his rivals.

However Rowland's "charisma" and "autocratic style" caused disquiet. In 1971 his merchant banker, the very reputable Warburgs, refused to represent Lonrho's interests. In 1973 his staid fellow directors staged a revolt, led by Sir Basil Smallpeice. Smallpeice's background could not have been more different to Rowland's. Educated at the Tudor foundation, Shrewsbury School, brought up in a classical environment in the days of Empire, he was typical of the kind of manager who was presiding over British industry. Rowland was quite outside his experience. "The irresponsibility of Mr Rowland," complained Smallpeice, "outweighed any benefit to be derived from his abilities and contacts." Among the "contacts" was Duncan Sandys (Winston Churchill's son-in-law and a former Minister of Defence), whom Rowland had appointed Chairman and favoured with $100,000 a year tax-free in the Cayman Islands.

More scandal emerged when Rowland's disregard of tax regulations was revealed. Ted Heath called Rowland's reckless methods "the unpleasant and unacceptable face of capitalism". However, Rowland was acceptable enough to his shareholders who, at a famous meeting, routed Smallpeice and his rebels with a massive vote of confidence in Rowland. The shareholders' confidence seemed inspired when over the next three years, and against the general industrial trend, Rowland trebled Lonrho's profits. Nor was Rowland worried by the revelations of the Department of Trade which denounced Lonrho's trading practices, including the claim that "the group had violated economic sanctions against Rhodesia" (*The Financial Times*).

In the late seventies Rowland bought *The Observer* secretly and overnight from its Californian owner, much to the horror of the

29 Somara Machel, leader of Frelimo, the guerilla movement which fought for the independence of Mozambique. Frelimo became the government of Mozambique in 1975.

30 Kenyan President Arap Moi. Like Machel, he was amongst Rowland's circle of influential friends.

paper's staff. *The Observer* had influence in Black Africa which suited Rowland's own interests there, and he also wanted closer access to the new Tory government under Mrs Thatcher.

Rowland's one disappointment in Britain was his failure to gain control of Harrods, the flagship of British commerce. When Harrods's appeal to the Monopolies Commission was upheld, the Commission's verdict stated that "Lonrho's management lacked depth".

But Rowland never relied on Britain alone. The oil crisis of 1973-74 was just the condition of market uncertainty which provided an opportunity for him.

He was probably right predicting that joint projects with Arabs and Africa would become the most important aspect of our business. [In 1975] Kuwaiti investors had bought 22 per cent of Lonrho, as a means to invest money in the Third World, particularly Africa. . . Rowland had cleverly become part of a critical new triangular relationship – between Arab capital, Western technology and Third World markets and products. (*The Changing Anatomy of Britain*)

Rowland may have caused much resentment; however, he can be seen as a catalyst on business practices in Britain.

The emergence of these global entrepreneurs was only one symptom of more fundamental changes in the British economy. Companies had to face far more intensive competition . . . with structures which were too rigid, too bureaucratic and too overmanned. (*The Changing Anatomy of Britain*)

Although differing in almost every other way, Rowland as much as Sinclair went against the grain of business expectations in the seventies – and both in their own way were signposts to the Thatcher years of the 1980s.

JOURNALISTS

There were moments in the seventies when the system of government, public accountability, even the social structure, seemed susceptible to radical change. From the extreme right, rumours of para-military coups d'état led by retired generals reached the press. By the late seventies disaffected left-wing groups such as Militant Tendency had infiltrated Labour councils whose leaders were disillusioned by the lack of direction and incapacity of Labour government.

With Britain increasingly dominated by the media, the journalist's role may have been more significant than ever before, especially in the fraught political and social circumstances. Tom Wolfe, the American pioneer of "new journalism", said the contemporary novelists had shirked social issues: "Journalists had inherited the mantle of the nineteenth-century realists." Outstanding among the journalists of their generation who inherited this mantle are the three featured here.

Christopher Booker and Paul Foot share some common ground: their background, education and their contributions to the successful satirical magazine *Private Eye*. They were Journalist of the Year award winners and both wrote with flair, precision and accessibility. Booker wrote revealingly on all aspects of the seventies from a relatively "neutral" position – in the sense his targets were the follies of government and planners, regardless of political shades.

Foot is far more of a political activist. On top of his commitment to a more just society through his work with the Socialist Workers Party, Foot is a virtuoso public speaker. His arguments for an alternative Marxist-based society are always provocative and stimulating. But after the mid-seventies, Foot's vision of a socialist democracy rarely attracted much support beyond a narrow, devoted base.

Jeremy Seabrook's journalism reached the very roots of ordinary people, often the victims of huge bureaucracies and insensitive practices by local authorities. His observations are sharp, melancholy sketches. Unemployment, anxiety and racial prejudice, the social implications of old age, the uprooting and dispersal of bewildered council tenants are the subjects of Seabrook's investigations. They are confused people, angry at the present and, sometimes, nostalgic for the past which is beyond recall. Then, there are the "Petes" (see page 43) who are aggressively determined to make good on their own terms and probably voted for the Conservatives in 1979.

Christopher Booker (1937-   )

Christopher Booker was born in Somerset; both his parents were teachers. He won a history scholarship to Shrewsbury School and went on to Cambridge. He was *Private Eye*'s first editor – in fact, its "presiding genius" for a while. A demanding colleague "who kept people till 4 a.m." to drive his copy to the printers, he was soon dismissed. He then wrote his book on the fifties and sixties, *The Neophiliacs*, which his colleague, the humorist

William Rushton, said was "his *Private Eye* stuff with all the jokes left out". Not that Booker's style of journalism was meant to be amusing. His classical background and communication skills enabled him to set contemporary issues in terms and values which are timeless. Not all these qualities fitted easily into the more relaxed tone of *Private Eye*.

"The Death of Progress" is how Booker describes the opening section of his perceptive book, *The Seventies*. He claims that the decade destroyed the twentieth century dream that

through science and technology, we should be able to unlock the "secrets of the universe" . . . master nature and thus create a materially secure and comfortable life for the majority of mankind . . . that, through drastic social and political reorganization, aided by the greater use of state planning, we should be able to create an entirely new kind of just, fair and equal society, [and], through the dismantling of all the old repressive "taboos" and conventions of the past – whether in social attitudes or the arts – individuals would be able to enjoy a much greater degree of freedom and self-realization. . .

Some time in the seventies a profoundly significant moment was passed in the history of mankind – the moment it became evident that, after all the advances of the previous 20 years, our societies were actually, in countless ways becoming less efficient . . . for all our computers, labour-saving devices and electronic gadgets, we were beginning in many ways to get less service, less benefit.

31 "There was a wide-felt revulsion against the deadening, destructive character of technology itself, its power to inflict untold harm on nature . . ." (Christopher Booker). Aftermath of the chemical plant explosion at Flixborough, in 1975.

Furthermore, the remorseless stripping of the earth's resources on which technology and prosperity depended was causing anxiety. The flow of British-owned North Sea oil (1975) was not inexhaustible.

The rate at which new oil reserves were being discovered was overtaken by the rate at which we were consuming oil. By the end of the decade that world energy crisis (which in the sixties had seemed little more than an environmentalists' "scare story") had already begun to become a reality . . . far from preparing the way for some Utopian future, it might well turn out before long to have been just a very short-lived phase in the story of mankind.

All kinds of people recognized that the "scientific and technological modes of relating man to nature and to the universe might in themselves have severe and potentially catastrophic limitations". Therefore, people came to regard the world's resources and wildlife with more sensitivity.

Booker had always been one of the severest critics of urban planners. In 1972, in collaboration with Bennie Gray, Booker wrote a series of newspaper articles on property deals which won him the Campaigning Journalist of the Year award. Booker exposed the corruption of a number of the property deals which were financed with "fantasy-money"; that is money spent today and earned

32, 33 The ugliness of city planning and the corruption of property dealers were frequent targets for Christopher Booker's outrage.

tomorrow. The money was never earned because these property companies and "fringe" banks went bankrupt in the 1974 recession.

He savaged the architectural "Modern Movement Dream".

Vast areas of cities had been transformed into inhuman moonscapes of tower blocks, set in a sea of dereliction. The millions of (mostly poorer) people who had been herded into the concrete Gulags of the new housing estates were victims of all attempts to realize the twentieth-century dream of Utopia. In the seventies it became clear how profoundly this version of the dream, like others, had failed. (*The Seventies*)

Peter Shore, the Environment Secretary, assured the 1976 International Habitat Conference that "Britain had paid off the bulldozer".

Booker saw the problems of the west reflected in struggles within Eastern Europe. Alexander Solzhenitsyn, a Nobel Prize winner (1970) and the most famous dissident writer, was expelled from Russia in 1974. His book *The Gulag Archipelago* (published 1974-78)

revealed to the world just how horrific had been the experience of Russia under Socialist totalitarianism . . . how the systematic policies of enslavement, extermination and genocide had amounted to the greatest crime in the history of humanity . . . wherever Marxist regimes had taken over during the seventies reports of slave camps and massacre trickled out. (*The Seventies*)

Solzhenitsyn's play *The Love Girl and the Innocent* (1976) was set in a Russian labour camp. It showed how political prisoners of conscience were treated appallingly while camp privileges and some devolved authority

were given to convicted murderers, thugs, and infanticides.

People's attitudes to Solzhenitsyn became more ambivalent once the lionizing faded. Some dismissed him as authoritarian, not unlike the regime which had exiled him: "a self-righteous prophet", "humourless and irritating", and to a few even a spy sent to undermine the fabric of the West by moral pressure where the threat of arms was ineffective. Booker clearly uses Solzhenitsyn's opinions on the "free world" to mirror British society:

the collective thinking of people, spiritual emptiness, the conformism and relentless triviality of the media . . . the extraordinary degree to which our society has come to place importance on rights rather than obligations . . . how legalistic our social relations have become, everyone operating to the "extreme limit" of the legal framework . . . in spite of material comfort inconceivable 30 years ago, how strained and unhappy so many people looked . . . the decline of courage by politicians, academics and social leaders. (*The Seventies*)

Booker's contribution to seventies journalism was to expose cant and superficiality in many forms – so his readers had the chance to reassess their values and expectations. Some of Booker's views are echoed by the historian Lawrence Le Quesne, in his book *After Kilvert*. Le Quesne agrees that individuals feel threatened by "The great brute corporations, government, business, trade unions" and adds

. . . something has indeed gone wrong with the world. . . The political use of murder by the million, nuclear weapons, the threat to the environment: these are things which threaten all men equally.

Paul Foot (1937-   )

Paul Foot has been dedicated to the ideals of the Socialist Workers Party (SWP) while operating, at various times, as a journalist on *The Sunday Telegraph* and *Private Eye* (1967-72), to which Foot's radical investigative journalism gave authority. In 1972 he won the Journalist of the Year award, and from 1972-78 edited the SWP magazine. Since 1979 he has had his own column in *The Daily Mirror*.

Foot comes from a Liberal background. His father, Lord Caradon, was a distinguished colonial administrator and UK representative on the United Nations. By the time he left Oxford University he was a "Tribunite" socialist and President of the Oxford Union. He seemed set on conventional politics much in the career pattern of his uncle, Michael Foot, whom Paul has always admired. However, he underwent a fundamental change in his political attitudes, which led him to a commitment to a radical reconstruction of British society outside mainstream politics.

It all began in Glasgow where Foot worked as a young journalist on *The Daily Record* in the early sixties.

I think I had always been a Marxist, I'd simply never heard of it until I went to Glasgow and looked around. The Marxist sects were very strong within the Labour Party in Glasgow. I was particularly attracted to the smallest sect, the International Socialists (IS). Mostly, they were exceptionally articulate and impressive young men and women, and their debates were hugely superior to the debates in Parliament. The youngsters were apprentices in the shipyards. They were people whose politics were part of their lives but had gained nothing from their politics. Their argument on Russia, on our society and the ebb and flow of the class struggle quite simply put my own opinions to flight.

By the time Foot returned to London in the late sixties his vision for society and the means

34 Paul Foot: his journalist experience in Glasgow's docklands changed his beliefs. "I went into a totally different kind of world for which neither Shrewsbury School, Oxford nor the army had prepared me."

to secure this aspiration were assured.

I was never a communist. To us in the IS the Russian Revolution had been lost – modern Russia was State Capitalism; a tyrannical, exploited society in which no socialist politics could survive. . . In Glasgow, over one New Year, I was duty journalist in the newsroom and read one of the greatest books written this century – Leon Trotsky's *History of the Russian Revolution.* I had to work out for myself the central Marxist argument; do you change society through the established means of electing Labour governments through Parliament and moving society to the left that way? Within weeks I was convinced by the argument. And I realized that the Labour Party was so entrenched within the capitalist system that I could never in any shape or form take political office or any other position of influence or power over people under this system.

Foot denounced the performance of Wilson's government (1964-70) and the 1974-79 Labour administration which confronted capitalist problems with capitalist solutions.

The distinguishing feature of all Labour governments, and the 1976-79 was the worst of them all, was their inability to deal with the powers they were elected to provide for the needs of the people who voted Labour. The reality is that the rich have all sorts of powers which they use all the time, nothing to do with powers in Parliament. By operating all together these people can trap a government into impotence. Even if a government is hostile to all these things there's precious little a government can do if all these groups combine to oppose it. And if government decides to soak the rich, as Healey promised, the institutions will send millions of pounds out of the country and tell the government they'll only bring the funds back if,

say, dividend restrictions are lifted. This was exactly what the IMF (page 22) intervention in '76 was all about.

In 1977 Paul Foot published *Why You Should be a Socialist*, which sold 44,000 copies. In this he set out the case for the SWP. "Britain is an extremely limited democracy," Foot wrote.

People vote according to where they live. It operates only in a small corner of society. In the areas which matter – in industry, finance, the civil service, the law-courts, the police force, the army, there is no democracy at all. Parliament doesn't challenge that power. The mass of officials, therefore, are completely unaccountable. They operate, not on behalf of society, but on behalf of one class, and there is no democratic machinery to control them. A few ordinary capitalists decide that architects must construct Centre Point [the office block in London] or Ronan Point [a council high rise which fell down]. They decide that physicists must work on nuclear weapons.

By contrast, the fundamental unit of workers' democracy is the workers' council based on the work-place. The workers' councils run through each part of industry and the services. The government is also made up of workers' representatives, elected through the councils, grouped this time on a regional basis, to a national Congress of Councils, which then elects its executive – the government. . .

Under [socialism] the broad decisions – hospitals or offices, saving or spending, pensions or aid to India – are taken by democratically elected councils. And once the broad decisions are taken, the technical decisions will still be left to people with the necessary skill and knowledge. All the thrust of socialist society will be towards the spreading of expertise and the enlargement of experts' social responsibility. . . Capitalism is the biggest "Brain Drain" of all, since it discounts the brains of about 80 per cent of the population.

35 The Unemployed Workers Union, Newton Abbot (1971): ". . . organized initially to grow and distribute vegetables. The Union is a people's organization, giving mutual benefits to members from their own collective resources."

36 "People come together and co-operate most at work, not at home – the workplace is a far better unit for a democratic system" (Paul Foot). The 1977 Grunwick dispute over unfair dismissals.

The years 1972-74 seemed to provide the promising conditions for a radical transformation of society.

I really believed there was going to be a cataclysmic upturn in society. In '68 students had forced concessions from University authorities. And now the miners' strikes humiliated and defeated the great Tory Party, [the miners'] leadership made the Labour leaders look such pale figures . . . management was in turmoil; government investment plans were changed . . . middle-class people became socialists overnight. . . The circulation of the SWP weekly soared to nearly 50,000, more than the *Tribune* and *New Statesman* combined. It was a very exhilarating time to be a socialist.

This heady enthusiasm gradually dwindled.

We'd generated this tremendous energy to get Labour into power to do the job it was elected to do for us. We didn't understand how quickly that great movement could evaporate under the aegis of a Labour government. The capitalist class, nervous as hell, was re-grouping; the Labour government left to itself was very susceptible to it. All Labour's policies were uprooted by powers which were much stronger than itself.

In 1978 Foot relinquished the editorship of the SWP weekly after a "vicious sectarian" dispute on the future direction of the movement. It was a dispiriting time. "I had given all my thirties to the SWP paper. I had no money, no job, no house and I was 41. I returned to *Private Eye* like a waif."

No editor approached him, though this could have been a measure of Foot's success with a paper and a movement which threatened "the Bourgeois" and Labour alike. Moreover, his book on immigration (1965) had alienated him further from Labour, although it consolidated his reputation as a direct, articulate and forceful scourge of the contemporary political and social scene.

Then, quite unexpectedly, in 1979 Foot was offered his own column in *The Daily Mirror*.

My column is not SWP propaganda. I intervene on behalf of the dispossessed, the deprived and the terribly poor against the rich who exploit them. I leave my readers to draw their own inferences. I'm still committed to the SWP; in fact my work with SWP makes me a better journalist and my journalism with the *Mirror* a better SWP member.

In 1980, Foot won The British Press Awards' Campaigning Journalist of the Year. In present political circumstances, it is hard to see his intriguing vision prospering. Few can dispute its objective of a fairer society in which Britain could be regenerated by freeing the disinherited, without necessarily harming the possessors. Nor does it reflect well on a society if it was true that

In 1975 social security "frauds" amounted to a loss to the government of £2 million. There were 13,350 prosecutions. In the same year tax evasions were estimated to have cost the government £1000 million. There were 126 prosecutions for tax evasion. (*Why you should be a Socialist*)

However, the British as a whole are not yet convinced that Paul Foot's socialist democracy would be less corruptible and more accountable if decision-making processes and destinies worked upwards from the place of work. Perhaps Foot can take comfort from his hero, and the subject of a book of his, the social revolutionary and poet, Shelley. Shelley's notions were thought to subvert the society he hoped to liberate, and his poetry was suppressed until after his death.

Jeremy Seabrook (1944-   )

Jeremy Seabrook comes from a Northampton family. Many of his ancestors worked in the town's historic boot and shoe industry, which used to employ half the town's labour force. Seabrook was the first in his family to go to university. He has worked in the BBC and taught handicapped children. While he was teaching with the Workers' Education Association, some of his lectures were printed in *New Society* to which journal, and *The Guardian*, he has since contributed.

In numerous ways Northampton provided a microcosm of similar towns in 1970s Britain. Their economy had been buoyant in the past, but was based too often on a single major industry – such as shipbuilding in Newcastle. These industries had declined, and by the 1970s Northampton's once thriving shoe industry employed very few people. The town was designated one of the second wave New Towns. The decline of the traditional industry, the dislocation of people's lives which followed New Town development and the emergence of new businesses with no local roots had social implications which were one of the challenges of the seventies. They resulted in fragmentation of self-contained communities where, "a quarter of the families had close relatives living in the same street, and many more had kinsfolk in one of the neighbouring terraces. . ."

The businesses of food processing, Barclaycard and the American Avon cosmetics were, according to Seabrook, outposts of

multinational corporations with remote control, a global economy and the mobility of capital. . . Formerly, the working class knew who the boss was, and where he lived. They may have hated him and been treated unjustly but their lives had a focus; they all had a sense of belonging. Now the working people didn't know who owned their company or for whom they worked. They could not put names to faces. The multinationalization of local industries confused people abominably. When the forces of your destiny are amorphous and invisible, people fall out among themselves – this was one of the stories of the seventies. You don't know where to turn your anger – you see social evils but don't know where the causes lie . . . a product of this condition is *The Sun* 'which plays on the susceptibilities of confused people who do not understand or have purchase on the society they live in. *The Sun*, reflects the brutishness of behaviour, a world full of depraved people; it's an ugly, almost medieval, litany of horror. . . A trade unionist said to me "We used to know we lived under capitalism; now we're told we live in society", indicating people neither know nor understand the cause of the malaise.

Jeremy Seabrook has documented many disaffected people who were victims of confusion in the face of frightening and mysterious events. One was a man of 60 whose home was demolished:

I spent five years fighting for my home and country; and what Hitler could not do, he (who is he?) can do with a stroke of his pen.

Seabrook records a similar experience of a woman of 55:

I saw it in the *Chronicle and Echo*. I couldn't believe it. When he got home I said, "The house is coming down". He said, "What do you mean?". I said, "It's in the paper". I couldn't eat. I couldn't sleep. I just felt sick.

Seabrook goes on to say:

The people in these streets are regarded as a regrettable, though inevitable, sacrifice to the general progress that is felt by local councils. . . Since most of the tenants grew up poor, the houses they now own represent no less an advance on the houses of their childhood than their own children's aspirations to private estate and detached houses. The achievement of a lifetime is suddenly declared to be derisory, unworthy (*New Society*)

Wandering Northampton streets and apologizing for living so long were "the old boot and shoe workers, an ugly and anomalous survival in a society that has discarded them", like old boots. One of Seabrook's characters is "Harry".

Harry died in what had been a workhouse, but is now a geriatric hospital . . . in his last years he discovered he could read and enjoy *War and Peace* and *Bleak House*. [Before] he would have regarded such things as frivolous and irrelevant. For 63 years he inspected animal skins for flaws. . . When his brother was drowned Harry indicated his mother's strongest emotion was probably relief that it represented three slices of bread a day less.

"Don't let anybody tell you poverty isn't a crime," he used to say, "it's a crime against the poor. Life was a bloody poor do. You sweat your guts out for a life time and then finish up with the rest of the rubbish." Of factory owners: "The only thing they give you is diphtheria"; of the working class struggle: "No carrion ever killed a crow, did it?". A suit of wood was the only one he could ever expect to be measured for. Harry never married. He often said, "A woman could find the raw place in a man quicker than a blow-fly". (*New Society*)

Once Harry did court a woman. When she discovered Harry had taken all their joint savings and put in nothing they separated. Years later she became paralyzed and Harry wheeled her everywhere.

Another of Seabrook's sketches takes place outside a primary school where a group of mothers waited to collect their infants.

"Says they played with plasticine again. They played with plasticine yesterday. They could stay at home and play with plasticine."
"Strikes me that's all they're ever going to do."
"They won't learn that way."
"They don't seem in a hurry to teach them anything."
"They reckon it has to come in its own time, no good trying to force it."
"Well if they wait for our Dawn, they'll wait till Doomsday."
"You can't expect kids to know what's good for 'em."
'They need somebody at the back of 'em geeing 'em up. I mean, I know that Gary's bright, but he's lazy, all kids are, it's natural."
"It makes me wonder what schools are for sometimes."
(*New Society*)

The target for the parents' unease is vague. Should the teachers be blamed; or the head, the Education Authority or the College of Education? Elaborating, Seabrook attributes the discontent to the pampering of children at home and at school.

Neither teachers nor parents are quite satisfied; and they chafe and fret at . . . maintaining a superseded discipline which society no longer exacts of its members.

These confused people often believe that they are "threatened" by ethnic minorities, and adopt racist attitudes:

This country, it's a paradise for all spongers and shirkers of the earth. Their countries wanted their independence from us, didn't they. They chucked us out, they thought they could paddle their own canoe, let them get on with it. We should chuck them out now. They are not our responsibility. (Man, aged 45)

Reflecting on such responses Seabrook wrote,

They attribute to the immigrants – or the young, the feckless, the idle and dissolute – the same characteristics formerly assigned to themselves by their betters. Even in this they emulate their masters. We lack the cultural vigour to devise new responses, and can only produce the traditional reaction, the cultural cliché, as nineteenth century people did to the Irish.

Another person described by Seabrook is "Pete", son of a boot operative. He saved £2000 in three years from labouring jobs by day and private, untaxed work at night. When his investments failed and he was in debt he started all over again.

I couldn't live on money I didn't earn. . . These people who don't want to work, they've got no intention of working as long as they've got all the welfare do-goodies propping them up . . . half the money I earn goes to them . . . Parasites. It makes you bitter. I need a lot of things, but I've got to sub all these people who can't look after their own family . . . eight kids, they only have them so as to get the family allowance. It's everybody's duty to look after his own . . . I shan't

37 Demonstration in West London after the death of the New Zealand teacher Blair Peach, killed by a truncheon blow while protesting against a National Front election meeting.

need anything from the state. I won't go loony – I'm too sharp. . .

Jeremy Seabrook believes consumerism to be an important and a corrupting influence on people who seemed to benefit from affluence. Some believe this argument is rather puritanical. Seabrook feels that the reduced control people have over their lives has been replaced by the purchasing power of money, which gives them the illusion that they're free. He goes on to say that

The seventies paved the way for a society in which poverty has become acceptable. Once you've got two-thirds who are doing well and one-third poor, then the poor are electorally [politically] expendable. . . The tendency for a more thorough subordination to the necessities of buying and selling was perhaps the most significant aspect of the seventies . . . it is the logical development of that process of industrialization that has now succeeded in industrializing even our humanity. . . If consumerism can't be sustained you'll get some very frightened people.

38 Bull Ring and New Street in Birmingham city centre during the reconstruction of New Street station. Note how the city centre has been re-designed around the car, not the pedestrian.

ARTISTS

"There were few, if any, writers after 1945 who could compare with D.H. Lawrence or James Joyce or Virginia Woolf," writes Arthur Marwick, who admits "it would be unwise to press the point too far." Many writers of the seventies had made their mark earlier, some as far back as the 1930s. Philip Larkin, Ted Hughes and Robert Graves were among the dominant poets of the sixties and seventies. The sculptor Henry Moore and painters Elizabeth Frink, David Hockney and Bridget Riley had established their reputations before the 1970s.

Few would dispute that Evelyn Waugh and the lesser known but perhaps more perceptive Anthony Powell were among the outstanding novelists of their generation. However, they followed the well-trodden tradition of observing English manners, prejudices and attitudes from a narrow social and national base. They were not sociological writers in the line of Charles Dickens or political writers such as George Orwell. John Fowles and William Golding are among very few who moved away to some extent from this tradition, as did the dramatists Harold Pinter and Tom Stoppard. These four were well known in the sixties.

Graham Greene's writings and opinions have made an impact on every decade since the Second World War. He is important, too, because he broke away from the English literary tradition. His subject matter crossed the frontiers of class and nationality. Greene reminds us that beyond Britain there were repressed groups fighting in the seventies for freedom, while the British were largely fighting for more money.

Malcolm Bradbury and Piers Paul Read adapted the historic British genre to the social issues of the time. In *The History Man* (1975), Bradbury exposes the shallowness and, in the end, corruption of "radical" university teaching.

The anxieties of middle class families are well presented in Read's *A Married Man* (1979). Determined to protect their assets from state plundering, the "married man's" family steal from and exploit the Welfare State. The family and like-minded people colonize a "chosen comprehensive", while the children of the working classes are relegated as before to the second-class schools.

Michael Tippett is, perhaps, unique. He possessed exceptional talent for his craft and he handled musical ideas which were accessible. Tippett explored the harsh realities of loyalty and commitment, and raised the political and social consciousness of his listeners. His music has the enduring qualities which people call classic.

David Bowie is another artist whose music struck a chord with both genders. His lyrics reflected many of the anxieties of young people in the seventies.

David Bowie (1947-   )

The story of successful pop stars can be bleak and sad. On the surface there is a dream-like quality when, suddenly and dramatically, a pop star is idolized by millions and earns so much money that there is scarcely anything that can't be bought – both material objects and people. At the heady pinnacle of pop-art success other things are lost on the way: personal relationships, a sense of values and even personality – so that reality is indistinguishable from fantasy. Traumas can follow the first successful live concert or album release. Then, the power factor is reversed for the pop star is faced with the anxiety of not disappointing the expectations of the fans, and the commercial requirements of the promoters.

People who knew David Bowie in the sixties were surprised at his meteoric rise to stardom in the seventies. Ronnie Ross, the jazz saxophonist who taught Bowie, said "He was quite an average sort of pupil, nothing out of the ordinary." During Bowie's involvement with the Arts Lab in Beckenham, one of the musicians, Roger Wootton, remembers Bowie;

rather fey [fanciful, odd], quiet, intelligent, hard to get to know, not giving of himself very much. To me, he seemed like an average folk-pop singer/songwriter. He was not particularly impressive live and, in fact, the audience weren't impressed with him. . . He was sort of evasive and appeared shy . . . . he had little charisma, no star quality and not a lot of talent, and it came as a big surprise when he became as successful as he was.

Bowie overcame his unease with an audience by sheer persistence and, probably, by the support of his perceptive wife, Angie.

39 David Bowie challenged accepted social frontiers. This is Bowie in his *Ziggy Stardust* guise.

I get very bored with reading how difficult he is and how cold he is. He's not like that. He's a fabulous guy and very funny, but it took a long time to put him in a situation where I felt he was at maximum "comfortableness", so that his shyness – and he was very shy – was overcome.

It was like all that ego-building which eventually turns into a monster. It was very necessary because he was so unsure. Not of his talent – he always knew he was good and what a good songwriter and performer he was – but he was nervous of audiences. The idea of touching people in the crowd or letting people touch him was something that had not occurred to him . . . but to be that beautiful and that remote you've got to get a crowd to touch him because that was what got them wild . . . . caused the hysteria and enthusiasm.

Behind Bowie's public diffidence there lurked a thrust and ambition. In the 1960s he wrote out of the blue to the millionaire John Bloom for backing: "if you can sell my pop-group like you sell your washing-machines, you're on a winner." Bloom passed the "cheeky" letter on to the agent, Leslie Conn, saying "I like the style . . . . give him an audition." Bowie performed at Bloom's wedding anniversary. It was a disaster. Bloom's elegant guests were shocked by the unkempt dress of the pop-group, and the blues-derived music mystified them. Bowie was hounded from the dais by an angry Bloom shouting, "get them out; they're ruining my party." Conn comforted a distraught and tearful Bowie.

I told the sensitive soul not to worry, and that I was quite impressed and would be interested in managing the band. That's how it began.

The adventurous *Space Oddity* (1969) was an interesting landmark in Bowie's development. His friend and record producer, Tony Visconti, thought Bowie

was cashing in on the moon-landing. David had come up with something that was extremely unoriginal.

The music was skilfully orchestrated, if not profoundly original. The lyric's storyline, however, explains quite a lot about Bowie's personality.

Roy Carr and Charles Shaar Murray write that

Space Oddity is a tale of the most crushing and profound alienation: Bowie's astronaut hero, Major Tom, achieves a lift off, looks back on the planet and decides to cut off all communication and never return. This theme of withdrawal was one to which Bowie would return on subsequent occasions, notably on the *Low* album where the retreat was into inner rather than outer space.

Space Oddity was only used on television coverage of the moonwalk once the American astronauts had safely returned to earth! Many of Bowie's album and song titles became household words. From *Ziggy Stardust* (1972) onwards the music is original and the lyrics enlightened. Often the themes are disturbing, intelligent and philosophical.

Once Tony DeFries became Bowie's manager and provided for his every whim, Bowie was able to concentrate on his music and art to the exclusion of everything, and everyone, else. His American tours became a triumph after a sluggish beginning.

He (Bowie) had started off in Cleveland playing to 3000 people. He went back within two months and played to 20,000 people. In Philadelphia, it was like the Beatles had arrived. There were fans everywhere and people chasing after him in the streets. It was all very exciting and again, because none of us has gone through it before, it was really wonderful to watch this happen and to be part of it. (Tony Zanetta)

Zanetta soon recognized the self-destructive power of mass-idolization,

. . . . by the second tour, I think it began to get decadent. Staying at the Plaza and ordering champagne whenever you wanted – it does something to you. The arrogance began to creep in . . . we were all living out this myth of Ziggy Stardust and treated him [Bowie] as if he was Ziggy Stardust. . . .

Diana Gillespie recalls the excesses of pop-world success,

Angie and I would ride around in a scarlet limousine with TV in the back and a bar and a huge black guy as our bodyguard in the front. It was outrageous.

Bowie needed the support and confidence of people he could trust. His wife, Angie, had always reassured him but their marriage was strained. DeFries, too, had been another on whom Bowie depended. However, Bowie's success meant that the management of his affairs had become more institutionalized and remote from the band. DeFries had set up a company called MainMan in New York. Lee Childers describes the problems which set in,

It all grew too fast all of a sudden. All of us had been promoted out of any efficiency that we might have had. I had a huge office on Park Avenue with a personal assistant, two secretaries and nothing to do. I use to pull the blinds, turn out the lights and sit in the dark in terror, thinking, "What am I going to do here? There's nothing for me to do."

Increasingly DeFries became so wrapped up with the management demands of MainMan that Bowie became neglected and, then, isolated. Bowie resorted to drugs.

He'd discovered cocaine with a vengeance. He was really living the rock star legend to the ninth degree. DeFries was very upset, he hated drugs . . . they just stopped communicating. (Zanetta)

They soon separated.

By 1973 the frenetic pace of pop-star life had gathered momentum. That year *Aladdin Sane* was released.

It was the first album that Bowie made from a position of stardom, and it was all obvious that the heat was on and that he was under pressure from fans, critics and business ("Hey man! Oh Henry, leave me alone . . .") The album is highly fragmented and even though it contains much

40 An older (and wiser?) Bowie, showing the stylish but clean-cut image he projected from the later seventies onward.

excellent material the whole is oddly unsatisfying. (Carr and Shaar Murray).

Even so, the advance orders nearly matched the first Beatles album.

After a successful 1973 tour of Japan and crossing Russia on the Trans-Siberian Express, Bowie gave 40 appearances in Britain. The tour was known as "The Aladdin Sane Retirement Tour". The tour finished at Earls Court when Bowie did indeed announce his retirement for

two or three years at least. . . I ran into a very strange type of paranoid person when I was doing *Aladdin Sane*, very mixed up people and I got upset.

One may wonder who it was who was paranoid.

Bob Marley's reggae was political as well as religious, his lyrics emphasizing the oppression of blacks by white society, or "Babylon".

Bowie is something of a puzzle. Of all the pop stars, he seemed to be in control of his destiny more than most. Often, it was he who abandoned, or threatened to, the music and style he'd created. Nor did he depend on pop music exclusively. He had always responded to creative stimuli outside his own field of music. George Orwell's *1984*, Bertolt Brecht, early-twentieth-century German painting, Buddhism, American poets such as Jack Kerouac – they all fascinated him. Once global success had conquered his shyness,

David was able to achieve through his own dynamic approach to things and his ruthlessness which included weeding out anyone who did not contribute to his own dream (Angie Bowie).

Bowie had always admired his father, whose death stunned him. His father was public relations officer with Dr Barnado's and Bowie admired the work of that organization.

He feels very strongly about the fate of children, the fate of people who are less privileged than he is. . . . The Band Aid example, and that entire vehicle of causing some good to be done, is an area where I am sure he will make his influence felt.

Bowie's behaviour on the suicide of his mentally ill step-brother, Terry, was surprising. *The Sun* declared:

Rock idol, David Bowie, was lashed by his aunt for snubbing his step-brother's funeral. Grief stricken Pat hit out at the millionaire singer saying "I hope God forgives you David – this is a tragic rejection!"

The Sun failed to report a desolate Bowie's inscription on the wreath he sent:

You've seen more things than we can imagine, but all these moments will be lost like tears washed away by the rain. God bless you; David.

Bowie's successful performance in the film *The Man Who Fell to Earth* (1976) coincided with a major change in musical direction, resulting in new backing musicians on the highly-regarded *Station to Station* album, and the experimental *Low, Heroes* and *Lodger*, a trilogy of 1977-79, recorded in Berlin. In Bertolt Brecht's *Baal*, Bowie identified with a lead part similar to himself – an artist with a non-conformist, anarchical attitude to the world. In *Baal*, and in *The Elephant Man*, Bowie won the admiration of experienced actors by his dedication and stage presence. Tony Visconti believed that "on stage he was magnificent and that was his real medium." He refused to withdraw from his acting commitments when John Lennon was shot and every cult-pop artist felt nervous that the same might happen to them.

One notion of pop heroes is that they are victims of consumerism and of a parasitic society dominated by newspapers which appeal to the base and perverted instincts of the people. Pop stars are vulnerable to scandles in their personal life, press exposures, and the fickleness of their fans once the music is no longer compelling.

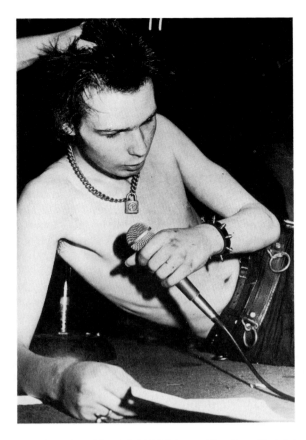

Bowie reflected in his songs, and especially the lyrics, the instability and insecurity of the seventies. By the end of the decade, he had emerged as the key link between the music of the sixties and the New Wave acts which sprang up in the wake of the Punk movement. Pessimism was something they shared: Bowie himself said

The world is doomed! We're not capable of making it any better – people just aren't going to have reasonable destinies.

However, a toughness and resilience seemed to be present in Bowie which enabled him to survive his "changes of personality", his family and social disruptions, a morbid view of the world, and perhaps, the opinion of Connor Egan, an eighties teenager, that "Bowie's albums may not sell now, but he can still fill a concert hall."

43 The Swedish group ABBA, winners of the 1974 Eurovision Song Contest and seventies superstars. The conventional looks and attitudes of the group reflected their easy listening but danceable music.

42 The Sex Pistols' Sid Vicious. The Sex Pistols' lyrics, music and behaviour outraged the public but delighted their fans, their single "God Save the Queen" becoming an unofficial No. 1 during the week of the Royal Jubilee in 1977. Vicious died from a drug overdose while awaiting trial on charges of alleged murder in 1979.

Perhaps because Bowie cared so much for Terry he couldn't face the funeral. Angie may come near the truth:

David adored Terry . . . and had a very good relationship with him. . . . I don't think it was a case of David didn't want to go. I don't think he didn't want to do something about it. He just looked at the problem and realized the magnitude of it. It was so enormous that to have got involved he really would have been working on a voluntary basis taking care of someone who had already been abused by the [Health] system from far too young an age when David was too young to have been able to do anything about it. . . .

Michael Tippett (1905-   )

In 1977 an exhibition to celebrate Michael Tippett's life and musical achievement was arranged. To mark that occasion Colin Davis, the conductor and musical director at the Royal Opera House, wrote his personal tribute to Tippett,

This exhibition is a way of saying 'Thank you' for the example you have set us of a creative mind true to itself in the face of the changing fashion of our uncertain times . . . . but most of all your faith that the workings of the intellect are as nothing without reference to the heart. (Letter in *A Man of Our Time*)

1977 was also the year that Tippett's masterly opera *The Ice Break* was first performed. Many people recoil from opera believing it to be elitist art with no meaning or entertainment value for ordinary people. Tippett's genius enabled him to break down the historic barriers around opera and make his operatic works accessible to all. Unlike many operas the words (which Tippett wrote himself) are as crucial to the artistic unity as the music, drama and dance.

Tippett's musical range embraces virtually every known form from small instrumental groups to his four operas. His early operas

received a mixed response. While the music critic, Martin Cooper, claimed Tippett's third opera *The Knot Garden*, "a triumphal example of musical theatre concerning itself with genuinely human values", *The Midsummer Marriage* mystified people at first. The world famous soprano, Joan Sutherland, was told by Tippett,

not to worry if I didn't understand. Leave the audience to work out the significance. The opera means what it says – nothing more!

The Ice Break, described as a "Modern Morality", is a microcosm of the seventies. Tippett takes human conflicts on individual and group levels which, though not new, were particularly violent in the decade. The theme is hope for mankind after closed minds have been opened; the subject-matter is reconciliation of opposites, group tensions, racism and stereotypes, personal identity and individual rebirth, generation conflicts.

Two of the central characters are Yuri, Russian-born but American-bred, and his father Lev, just released after 20 years in Russian camps. Lev can't understand why there is "comradeship and passion for life in the camps and nullity and empty conformism in the world of his release." At the beginning of this taut, short (75 minutes) opera Yuri's brutality to his father is horrifying; "every guy has a gun here," he says and taunts his father for allowing himself to be locked away for 20 years. On one occasion Yuri rants at Lev, "What have you come here for?"

After a moving reconciliation when Yuri is healed of his terrible injuries in a race-riot, which he partly provoked, and of his unkindness to his father, Lev says, "Yet you will always be brought forth again, glorious image of God, and likewise be maimed, wounded afresh, from within or without."

Michael Tippett was born in London, the second son of a retired lawyer who became proprietor of a hotel in Cannes, in the South of France. Tippett was educated at Fettes, the famous Scottish school, and Stamford Grammar School. At the Royal College of Music he was taught by Adrian Boult and Malcolm Sargent. It was some years before Tippett could live by his music alone. He followed the time-honoured practice of part-time teaching, though at one level Tippett was a teacher all his life.

In the 1920s Tippett tells us,

I know now that my life lay in artistic creation. I scarcely considered any of the great contemporary events which seemed to lie outside my musical needs.

However, as the forces of fascism and dissent began to cloud the political scene of the 1930s, Tippett became more conscious of, and committed to, the need for music to reflect life's harsher realities.

In 1932 Tippett had hiked North to bring music to the unemployed miners and had been horrified by the "undernourished children" and conditions of the poor. He wrote in *Moving into Aquarius*

The Spring (coming of Peace) was false, and that in fact it was still Winter. For the majority of my countrymen perhaps there had never been a Spring at all. Had I the right to turn away from such reality, to shut myself up to write abstract music?

One of his most famous works, a secular oratorio called *A Child of Our Time* (1939-41), answered this question. The work was inspired by the assassination of a German diplomat by a Jewish boy, which is exploited by Nazi Germany to unleash a savage pogrom [organized massacre]. "I felt I had to express collective feelings", wrote Tippett about his oratorio,

and that could only be done by collective tunes such as Negro spirituals, for these tunes contain a deposit of generations of common experience.

The *Times* wrote,

44 Michael Tippett looked beyond the narrowness of individual cultural and ethnic relationships in his opera *The Ice Break*.

Tippett has succeeded to a quite remarkable extent in creating a powerful work out of a contemplation of the evil abroad in the world of yesterday and today.

In 1940 Tippett was director of music at Morley College. On grounds of conscience he refused to enlist in the army. He spent three months in prison in spite of Dr Vaughan Williams's appeal in the *Times*

I think Tippett's pacifist views entirely wrong, but I respect him very much for holding them so firmly.

In Wormwood Scrubs prison Tippett wrote,

I was now myself an outcast. It seemed indeed that this particular split between myself and society was part of the continuous and wider split between the artist affirming what he believes to be absolute values, and society which seemed bent on destroying itself.

Throughout the seventies Tippett had a close rapport with America. The Chicago Orchestra commissioned his *Fourth Symphony* (1976) which Sir Georg Solti (former musical director at Covent Garden) conducted the following year, and his music transcended the cultural and racial divisions in the American continent:

Students have been seen at concerts wearing sweaters bearing the slogan "Turn on to Tippett!"

When the Dallas Symphony Orchestra staged a 56 hour fund-raising marathon programme, one incentive was to play music from the most popular composer voted by the donors. Tippett won the most votes, ahead of Beethoven and Mahler.

Looking back at the "huge and world-shattering events" of his lifetime he contemplated his role in the book *Moving Into Aquarius*,

fundamental to our civilization is to create images from the depths of the imagination . . . Images of vigour for a decadent period, images of calm for one too violent, images of reconciliation for worlds torn by division. And in an age of mediocrity and shattered dreams, images of abounding, generous, exuberant beauty.

The young people who sing that great hymn of affirmation, Blake's "Jerusalem", are not so naive as to imagine that they will in fact build it any more than all mankind will be brothers. Yet there is a momentary vision of a possibility.

Tippett's music and his undaunted spirit keeps that possibility alive. If so much of the seventies is easily forgotten, Tippett's contribution went well beyond his musical legacy – it was a testament to humanity. That *The Ice Break*, a modern opera, provoked such excitement was one of the more encouraging and enduring experiences of the seventies.

OBSERVERS

There are always people who are exceptionally talented and respected by their colleagues, whose insights into their times can seem so much more perceptive than those in power. For understandable reasons, these people prefer not to seek public office. At least they remain their own selves, and avoid being dominated by the conformist demands of institutions. In short, they are unknown people with unusual minds.

Despite being the focus of much media attention, teenagers also remain observers – but often observers with a great deal to say about the world they are growing up in.

Peter Bush (1946-   )

Peter Bush has written a vivid and moving family history:

My paternal grandfather was a shepherd in a Lincolnshire village. His wife picked potatoes, was a "community" midwife and had 16 children in their tied cottage. He fell ill one Christmas and they were evicted by the Conservative landowner. My father, his mother and elder sister lived in a shed for a year (a kind offer from a neighbouring Liberal landowner) and grandfather went to the workhouse transformed into a paupers' hospital until they were allocated a council house where I was born.

My maternal grandfather was a carpenter and lived in a five-storey tenement in Sheffield. They also had 16 children. It was an industrial working-class district of miners, steelworkers, Irish and Jewish immigrants. Help was given to striking miners and repaid with coal. Grandmother wrote letters for illiterate neighbours. . .

Dad returned from the war (France, Egypt: the working-class is forced into international travel for the democratic purposes of war) determined to change society and not return to the thirties.

He established a trades union in his workplace and the region, and helped form the Trades Council. . .

My father would talk about constant battles over pay and conditions. A six o'clock morning shift at the age of 60 meant getting up at four-thirty and arriving home at six thirty in the evening. The disruption of family and social life was such that at retirement my parents had become strangers as far as living together was concerned. That *is* cultural deprivation.

[Nearby] was Royce Road, the Council dumping ground for "problem" families . . . friends at primary school but those friendships would not survive the 11-plus divide. . .

From Grammar School Peter went to Cambridge.

The public schoolboy next door left after one day and jumped from a train. Across the corridor was the Christian Marxist son of a South African bishop, and upstairs a lover of hunting and the aristocracy frequently cracked his whip – he is now under-secretary for privatizing the NHS. After a bout of aestheticism, my favourite lecturer became Raymond Williams and my country of preference became Spain. I began to enjoy classical music.

At Oxford University Peter "first met West Indian parents and youths, and the hatred of college society for anyone who stepped outside the academic community." He also got his doctorate for research on the Spanish novelist, Benito Galdos, and met his future wife, Julia, a distinguished historian.

In 1973 I joined the staff of a school in North London which had 1200 pupils with a large number of Greek and Turkish Cypriot pupils, a good many from council estates but a few from professional homes.

While always closely involved with classroom teaching, Peter held senior management jobs in a variety of London schools, including the flagship of comprehensives, Holland Park, and most recently the innovative Stanctonbury Community School in Milton Keynes. From this position Peter was uniquely placed to observe a critical stage of the comprehensives' evolution. Peter recalls that there was

a critical shortage of teachers in the early seventies. The headteacher sent a letter to all the parents appealing for anyone they knew who could teach to come forward and teach for a couple of hours a day! Then came falling rolls, school mergers, people going through traumas in losing jobs and status, cuts in resources and now the Baker reforms . . . re-structuring, more changes, more teachers undermined.

In spite of this turmoil, the real issues of education were not lost sight of, nor was the level of debate diminished. The reconciling of imaginative teaching to traditional school management was one issue which Peter confronted at his Haringey school in North London.

45 Children from many ethnic backgrounds pose for a class photograph in a West London primary school.

"The traditional head liked having creative teachers who were not traditional; she realized their teaching carried the students." Complications arose when innovative teaching made demands on inflexible school management.

Creative teaching and traditional school leadership can co-exist. But once teachers began thinking of collaborating across subject boundaries and raised the issue with the deputy heads, this raised issues with the organization of, for instance, the timetable. . . The same timetable was carried through from one year to the next. If you want curriculum development, which may mean subject integration, you must have a school leadership which responds to it.

Peter recalls staffroom discussions on whether language should be toned down to help the less able and literate pupils. Peter strongly opposed the belief that "working class language was anything but enriching or that students could not grasp ideas." Most heartening was that the History Department agreed with Peter and "a large number of 14-year-olds chose history as an option after completing a very successful course on World Revolution."

In 1978/79 Peter was head of English in southern Spain in a market town.

My return was to the London dockside, and a working-class girls' school whose senior staff stood for standards and streaming. When asked why years of rigid streaming from day one of year one had not produced a flow of girls into higher education, the same established staff replied that one could not expect much from "dockers' daughters". There were few links with the community, no multicultural education and no music or drama. Standards, on the other hand, were much talked about. Some girls from Jamaica Road and thereabouts did stay with families in southern Spain and did welcome Spanish girls back in their homes.

The long-awaited Bullock report stated that "no child should leave his or her culture on the threshold of the school" but not until about 1979 was there a multi-cultural

"consciousness" in schools. Hitherto, it had been left to the awareness and perceptions of individual teachers.

The focus of education was mono-cultural. Many parents communicated with the school through their sons and daughters acting as interpreters. . . In Haringey, teaching largely ignored the one-third students who were Greek and Turkish speakers. One change was that a number of teachers became interested in the white working-class communities, and in the stories of Midland and Northern working-class families. Teachers in comprehensives thought that the white working-class children should be given space in an often traditional curriculum.

Equal opportunities was not a watering down of standards. A lot more students in this school went on to higher education who would not have done in the old secondary moderns. One problem was how far should teachers influence students against their cultural background. I had a number of sixth form students who were very able linguists from Greek speaking families who wanted to go to university. Higher education did not enter into their family tradition, or if it did the family wanted London University. They weren't keen on a university outside London which I thought would be more interesting for them.

Peter is in a real sense a community leader. His education philosophy transcends neighbourhood and, indeed, national frontiers. Hundreds of pupils from London Docklands, North and West London have benefited by accompanying Peter to Spain.

[Spain] gave me experience of the conditions which led illiterate peasants to fight for socialism and anarchism and to massive seasonal migrations as well as semi-permanent emigration to western Europe.

This social pattern is the subject of the book *Campos de Nigar*, by the Spanish writer Juan Goytisolo, which Peter edited and introduced (1984) and which reflected the lot of some immigrants in Britain (especially from Morocco) in the 1970s.

46 Agricultural worker Manolo cracks almonds for Peter Bush (right) and children in Archena, Murcia. Many Archena families have friends in England as a result of school exchanges.

In reality, they escaped from starvation to work in northern Spain (and North Europe) and their remittances to their families were then redirected by the banks to the north so that more Catalan or Basque entrepreneurs could open factories . . . for more migrant workers from the south. Export of labour was one of the pillars of the so-called Francoist economic miracle.

This generation of poor Spaniards now aspire to Higher Education.

In spite of disquiet about comprehensive schools from some quarters, Peter's vision kept the comprehensive conviction alive in the face of dispiriting and often badly informed criticism. Above all, he pointed out that education is for the whole community and extends well beyond the school gates.

Annabel Maunsell (1940-   ) and Jeffery Maunsell (1936-   )

Annabel and Jeffery Maunsell lived in London throughout the 1970s. Annabel is an artist who studied at Chelsea School of Art during the early seventies.

I did not attend College until our children were aged five and seven, and at primary school. Although commonplace now, it was unusual in the seventies to be a full-time female art student with school-age children. I took a degree in sculpture and went on to do an MA in print-making. I now work as a painter and printmaker. For a woman the 1970s was an important decade.

Jeffery does not agree with Christopher Booker that the 1970s was the most important decade of the twentieth century (page 33).

It does not compare with the forties (Second World War) or the decade of the First World War.

The sixties had a focus, although I don't accept all the clichés about the "swinging sixties". All this was over-romanticized (with hindsight) in the seventies. Few dates stand out in the seventies as, for instance, the Kennedy/Khruschev confrontation over the Cuban nuclear missile bases and President Kennedy's assassination in the sixties, though the oil crisis did affect our lives. Events, anyway, don't fall neatly packaged into decades. The general public have probably still not realized that higher standards of living are illusory.

Jeffery is a solicitor. Justice is one measurement by which people judge the level of civilization. The flaws in British Law do not elude Jeffery.

Justice does not exist. Only fools, paupers or the very rich can afford to litigate (go to law). Wealthy companies, who can use litigation as an

47 Jeffery and Annabel Maunsell, living through the seventies with perceptive and thought-provoking views.

48 'Jason', by Annabel Maunsell.

adjunct to commerce, dominate. They can oppress the individual with threats and pressures of a law suit and costs. The individual is led to capitulate regardless of the merits because he cannot afford to go the whole way.

Before Jeffery qualified in Law he worked for a short time in Independent Television after leaving Marlborough College, where he was one of the best rugby players of his time. As a schoolboy he played for the famous London club, Blackheath, for a short while until an injury ended his playing days prematurely. The irony was not lost on Jeffery that his opponents that day were St Mary's Hospital.

The Maunsells bring their own insights to bear on most things. Once, at a party in the mid-seventies, the talk ranged over contemporary moral attitudes. An elderly man present said that on principle he would never again see his daughter-in-law, who was in the process of getting divorced from one of his sons. "On the same principle," Jeffery remarked, "no doubt you won't be seeing your son again!"

Both feel people would probably get on better without interference from politicians. Certainly the performance of most seventies politicians did little to dispel their conviction. Within a few years the three leaders of the main parties left office, one in disgrace (Jeremy Thorpe), another in defeat (Edward Heath) and, in Wilson's case, for no obvious reason.

"Politicians, to remain in power", Jeffery says,

need to dupe the voters that at each election they will bring increased benefits and improvements in their living standards. This process cannot continue . . . because the country's, and the planet's, resources will not permit it. What the politicians had to contrive . . . was a great bump downwards into a trough so that the whole process could start again with the political leaders trying to outbid each other with promises to the electorate.

Elaborating on the crisis of the world's

resources, Annabel observed,

We began to realize that the earth's resources were likely to run out. It was a pincer movement: either we exhaust our resources, or we self-destruct; for example, nuclear war or ozone depletion or accidental nuclear disaster. Graft on to this the variation of a political or nationalist madman with a finger on the nuclear trigger. . .

The children of the 1970s were the first generation to accept as a part of their normal life that the world could end by one of these methods within their lifetime. Previously, mortality would sink in at about 30 or 40; now it could be understood by a five-year-old. They were told in the classroom that there was a bomb which could destroy the world. The difference between war in the 1940s, as waged and understood by our parents, and as now envisaged by their grandchildren, is reflected in films such as *Hope and Glory, Tora! Tora! Tora!* and *War Games.*

Jeffery reflected

Everything seems to have become focused on computers as the solution to all problems. They would solve business problems; space would be conquered. It became obsessive. Computers and word-processors do not cure business or commercial problems. They create an illusion of efficiency, and much business for their manufacturers.

In medicine there were more moral and ethical questions thrown up by medical science (page 5) being way ahead of human understanding.

Throughout the past 25 years a strong feeling prevailed that anything emanating from Soviet Russia was either designed like chess strategies to be or was likely to end up being a trap that would undermine the fabric of the West. The West was unsurpassed in undermining its own moral fabric unaided. The trade unions were in the ascendancy and had been exploiting their position for many years . . . (since 1979) Mrs Thatcher has called the tune. She has used every excuse to bring in legislation to curb the unions. The pendulum has swung too far the other way.

Alexi Harden (1960-   )

Alexi (Alexandra) Harden was a teenager in the 1970s. She was born in Brighton and moved from London to the Home Counties at five years old.

Alexi's adolescence was stable and positive under the benign care of cultured, enlightened parents. Throughout the seventies Alexi kept a diary on which the following reflections are mostly based.

In many ways I grew up in privileged circumstances which were not typical with less fortunate families. . . My daily life was an endless round of music and ballet lessons, Brownies, riding lessons, friends for tea, family holidays and outings to the theatre and cinema. In 1972 one could still picnic on the stones at

Stonehenge, and sit on the great chalk giant at Cerne Abbas. Unfortunately, these great English monuments are now fenced off.

Clearly, Alexi's parents were involved and encouraging but neither too intrusive nor destructively critical. When she was about 16 Alexi told her parents she was going out to busk (play music on the street for money) in High Wycombe. Many parents would veto such an idea. "What I didn't know", Alexi says,

was that my parents were so entertained by the idea that unknown to me and my musical friends they were watching from a distance. They were also amused when two policemen moved us along explaining we were contravening a law dating back to the Napoleonic Wars. We played the Beatles, me on the guitar, and collected £2.50.

Though naturally anxious as boy friends came along, Alexi's parents "never nagged me to be home by ten, so I usually returned by the time I'd told them".

The political dramas were observed by Alexi with detachment,

power cuts (1972) meant no electricity and more importantly, no *Dr Who*. The crisis was somewhat averted by the glamour of candlelight during the winter evenings. The television epic *War and Peace* ended (1973) and the three day working week was born. Picasso died, with me grandly thinking I could have painted better pictures at kindergarten.

Fashion has always been an obsession with young people, but Alexi was not a slave to teenage styles.

The decade opened with a bang, literally, as I broke my arm. To cheer me up my mother bought me a trouser-suit, whose flared trousers with matching jacket were the height of fashion. Clothes for men and women were completely unisex – always flared trousers or "bell-bottoms" and shirts with huge pointed collars. After the Beatles . . . men started to wear their hair long, which never looked clean, and still harked back to the hippies of the flower-power era.

Jeans, too, became widely worn; by 1979 American manufacturers were making jeans in Russia. Some fashions, including pop music and films, reflected a nostalgia for bygone eras and a general uncertainty about the present and the future.

Alexi's diary notes among others the following events:

Wilson formed the first minority government for 40 years (1974). . . The first non-Italian Pope since 1522 was elected (1978) – rather dramatic as the previous one had died suddenly. The Apollo moon landings were shown live early in

the morning – we all ate our cornflakes in front of this extraordinary event, so breakfast television came early into our home. The country went decimal (1971), and nobody had to do awful sums in £ s d any more. The Common Market agreement was reached and we felt very continental for a while, except we still drove on the left. 1971 was Hi-Tech year at home with the arrival of a Kenwood Chef food mixer, a freezer and a colour television.

Our dentist had innovative ideas about the benefits of direct fluoride application for under 16 year olds . . . it tasted revolting, but would apparently stand our teeth in good stead for the future – quite true so far!

The cinema made a big impression on Alexi:

Our family car (1970) was a VW Beetle, so we were taken to see *The Love Bug*. This was the start of a great personal interest in films and the cinema – films grew better as I grew older, or perhaps I enjoyed them with progressively greater maturity.

For the first time in 20 years attendances rose. Better films had to be made to compete with television, and the huge Odeons of the fifties were redesigned into smaller auditoriums which allowed viewers a choice of, perhaps, four films under one roof.

49 A still from Stanley Kubrick's film *A Clockwork Orange*.

Many popular teenage crazes, like skateboarding, started in America. Roller skating returned and by combining with disco-dancing created the new art of roller-disco. Alexi recalls two other crazes,

At school everyone wandered from one craze to the next: Slinkey was a giant spring which would walk downstairs; and ker-knockers which were two hard plastic balls suspended like pendulums from a handle which could be crashed together. These were eventually banned after some of the balls had shattered and sent dangerous splinters flying.

Alexi is an accomplished musician,

Classical music has always been a part of my life, and I badgered my parents into taking me to see the cellist, Paul Tortelier, as the first of my concerts. [By 1975] I began regular lessons with the pianist, the late Albert Ferbar. As a result my energies were channelled away from the various pop groups. Many of my friends lived and breathed pop music, and professed undying love for David Cassidy, Donny Osmond and the like. *Blue Peter* buried (1974) a lot of contemporary goodies outside Television Centre, not to be opened until the year 2000. This kind of thing had most 13-14 year olds more gripped than the Rolling Stones ever managed.

Exams recur in Alexi's diaries:

1976 chiefly remembered for the hottest summer in 100 years, most of which I spent in the exam room doing my O levels . . . 1977, more exams – grade VIII piano this time and a school performance in the Purcell Room at the Festival Hall. Opera was beginning to take a hold of me and we performed *Dido and Aeneas* at school.

'While Virginia Wade', writes Alexi,

was winning Wimbledon everybody was celebrating the Queen's Silver Jubilee (1977) which underlined a love for anything royal. The street party tradition and the lighting of a chain of beacons around the country were revived everywhere.

1975 was Alexi's

first year of striking out on my own. Our school arranged German penfriends and I went abroad for the first time to visit my correspondent. I also went to Italy on a working holiday with a family, and started earning at home through baby-sitting – these were popular trends.

Political terrorism overshadowed the 1970s.

I went to boarding school amidst the tragedy of the Munich Olympics (1972) when 11 Israeli athletes were murdered by Arab terrorists. I was present with the silent mourning crowd at Mountbatten's funeral procession [killed by the IRA] – the most moving part was the traditional reversal of arms, with his boots placed pointing backwards in the stirrups of his riderless horse (1979).

By 1979 Alexi was poised for a university career.

Working in Geneva. . . Much debate on the merits of the gap year between school and university. I wanted to see a different country, but could not escape English politics – Mrs Thatcher won the General Election and all the Swiss seemed to think I somehow knew all about it.

As it happened, Alexi's plans for university were overtaken by her decision to get married. She now lives in Yorkshire with her husband and two young children, where Alexi teaches music.

50 Saved! Apollo 13 astronauts return safely to Earth.

DATE LIST

1970

April — US Apollo 13 space mission fails. Astronauts survive.

June — Conservatives win General Election; Edward Heath becomes prime minister.

1971

February — Rolls Royce collapses. Decimalization introduced.

March — One-day strike by 1.5 million engineers in protest against Industrial Relations Act.

June — Parliament votes to join European Economic Community (EEC). Value Added Tax (VAT) on certain consumer goods introduced.

August — Internment without trial in Northern Ireland. Worst street riots in Ulster for 50 years. First British soldier killed.

1972

January — Miners' strike. Unemployment reaches 1 million. Reginald Maudling, a Conservative cabinet minister, resigns because of corrupt business transactions. Unrest in Ulster increases – British troops kill 13 civilians on "Bloody Sunday".

March — Direct Rule imposed on Northern Ireland from Westminster.

August — 40,000 Asian-Ugandans expelled and settle in the UK. 1.6 million people visit Tutankhamun exhibition at British Museum.

September — 32 unions suspended by the TUC for registering under the Industrial Relations Act. Free Birth Control.

1973

January — Britain joins EEC. Vietnam ceasefire agreement.

March — Referendum in Northern Ireland votes overwhelmingly to retain constitutional links with Britain.

October — Arab-Israeli War cuts oil supplies to West.

November — Major oil price increases by the oil exporting countries (OPEC). Miners, railmen, electrical and power workers ban overtime.

December — Emergency measures to conserve fuel: 50 mph speed limit, temperature control in offices, 3-day working week.

The Sunningdale Agreement; an attempt to bring political peace to Northern Ireland by setting up a Council of Ireland.

1974

January — End of Direct Rule from Westminster in Northern Ireland. Loyalists expelled from N.I. Assembly after angry exchanges.

February — Miners strike. Heath calls General Election. No party wins clear majority. Heath enters abortive coalition talks with Liberals.

March — Harold Wilson forms minority Labour government. End of 3-Day Week and miners strike.

May — State of Emergency in Northern Ireland due to Protestant opposition to Sunningdale Agreement: N.I. Assembly suspended and Direct Rule restored.

July — Heath's industrial relations legislation repealed. Mainland bombings by IRA. Casualties in Birmingham and Guildford pubs are 26 killed and 190 injured. Prevention of Terrorism Act proscribes IRA and gives police wider powers.

October — General Election gives Labour an overall majority of 3. 'Social Contract' comes into force. Solzhenitsyn expelled from Russia.

December — Government aid to British Leyland.

1975

February — Margaret Thatcher succeeds Heath as leader of the Conservative Party.

March — Meriden Motor Cycle run by workers' cooperative. International Women's Year. Sex Discrimination Act. The Children's Act.

April — Government invests £1400 million in British Leyland over 8 years.

May — Scottish *Daily News* published by workers' cooperative.

June — Referendum gives two-to-one majority for staying in EEC.

July — Anti-inflation policy: £6 per week limit on pay rises until August 1976.

November — Britain applies to IMF for £975 million loan.

December — End of internment without trial in Northern Ireland. Britain receives her first supplies of North Sea Oil.

1976

March	Harold Wilson resigns as Prime Minister.
April	Callaghan succeeds Wilson as Prime Minister.
May	Jeremy Thorpe resigns Liberal leadership.
June	Britain secures £3 billion standby loan from overseas banks. Race Relations Act.
July	David Steel elected Liberal leader.
September	Government seeks £2.300 million loan from IMF.
December	Government secures IMF loan on condition public spending is slashed by £2.500 million, indirect taxes are increased and BP share is sold.

1977

January	Bullock Report on industrial relations, recommends worker-directors.
March	Liberal-Labour (Lib-Lab) pact defeats Conservative motion of no confidence in the Labour government.
June	Britain celebrates the Queen's Silver Jubilee.
July	Trade Union demonstrations at Grunwick factory in support of workers' claim for union recognition.
August	National Front march provokes street violence in London.
September	National Front march in Manchester banned. Launching of Freddie Laker's Skytrain cheap flights.

1978

August	Lib/Lab pact dissolved.
November	TUC General Council refuses to endorse government's 5% pay limit.
December	"Winter of Discontent": severe breakdown in government economic and social policies as public sector employees strike for substantial wage settlements.

1979

March	Referendum in Wales and Scotland renounces Devolution plans. Government defeated in no-confidence vote for first time since 1924. General Election called.
May	Conservatives win General Election. Mrs Thatcher becomes first British woman Prime Minister.
December	Employment Bill on picketing, secret ballot and closed shop aims to reverse TU power by making its leadership more responsive to, and representative, of its members. Peace in Rhodesia, soon to become Zimbabwe. Lord Soames appointed governor to supervise elections which will end minority white rule.

Dockland

Cranes standing still, no work for them
No movement, a monument to times past.
Silhouette outlined against a London sky.

Their reflection, mirrored in the waters
   of a silent dock.
Casting their shadows across the decks
   of pleasure yachts.

Like a cancer spreading, with unchecked
   speed,
Wharves, warehouses closed overnight
Transformed, renovated
Not for people who have no place to live,
But for those who with obscene ease,
Sail their yachts whenever they please,
Leaving them moored outside their second
   homes.
It's all a part of our social disease.

Docks closed,
Once where dock workers played their part,
Shifting cargo, keeping London alive.
Now silence reigns, it is supreme,
Thrusting aside this industrial scene.

Gone now, this way of life,
Testimony to the power of those few,
Whose decisions carry far and wide,
Eroding, encroaching, changing the
Character of our riverside.

Bernie Steer (1975)

Bernie Steer was one of the five dockers who was imprisoned for defying Edward Heath's Industrial Relations Act (page 14).
Kenneth Baker, Education Secretary, included this poem in an anthology he edited. He pointed out over-manning and restrictive practices also contributed to the decline of the docks.

BOOKS FOR FURTHER READING

Books about the 1970s

Christopher Booker, *The Seventies*, Allen Lane 1980

Peter Bush, *Class, National Culture & Individual Identity*, University of London, Centre for Multicultural Education 1985

Roy Carr and Charles Shaar Murray, *Bowie*, Eel Pie Publishing 1981

Barbara Castle, *The Castle Diaries 1974-76*, Weidenfeld 1980

R.H.S. Crossman, *The Diaries of a Cabinet Minister 1975-77*, Weidenfeld, 1979

Bernard Donoghue, *The Conduct of Policy under Harold Wilson and James Callaghan*, J. Cape 1987

Paul Foot, *Why you should be a Socialist*, Socialist Workers' Party 1977

Jack Jones, *Union Man*, Hodder 1978

Jerry Juby (Ed.), *In Other Words – David Bowie*, Omnibus Press 1986

David and Maurice Kogan, *The Battle for the Labour Party*, Fontana, 1982

Laurence Le Quesne, *After Kilvert*, OUP 1977

Arthur Marwick, *British Society since 1945*, Penguin 1982

Keith Middlemas, *Politics in Industrial Society*, Andre Deutsch 1979

Anthony Sampson, *The Changing Anatomy of Britain*, Hodder/Coronet 1983

Robert Taylor, *The 5th Estate: British Unions in the Modern World*, Routledge 1978

Hugh Thomas, *History, Capitalism and Freedom*, (with Introduction by Margaret Thatcher), Centre for Policy Studies 1979

Michael Tippett, *Moving into Aquarius*, Paladin Books 1974

Philip Ziegler, *Elizabeth's Britain*, Newnes 1986

SOME NOVELS OF THE 1970s

Richard Adams, *Watership Down*

Beryl Bainbridge, *Sweet William*

J.G. Ballard, *The Unlimited Dream Company*

Malcolm Bradbury, *The History Man*

John Le Carre, *Tinker, Taylor, Soldier, Spy*

Len Deighton, *Bomber*

J.G. Farrell, *Troubles*

Michael Frayn, *Sweet Dreams*

Frederick Forsyth, *Day of the Jackal*

John Fowles, *Daniel Martin*

William Golding, *Darkness Visible*

Graham Greene, *The Honorary Consul*, *The Human Factor*

V.S. Naipaul, *A Bend in the River*

Piers Paul Read, *A Married Man*

Anthony Powell, *Books do furnish a Room*

Paul Scott, *Staying On*

Alexander Solzhenitsyn, *The Gulag Archipelago*

John Updike, *The Coup*

Fay Weldon, *Praxa*

SOME FILMS OF THE 1970s

All the President's Men
Annie Hall
Butch Cassidy and the Sundance Kid
A Clockwork Orange
Cabaret
Death in Venice
Diamonds are Forever
Enter the Dragon
The Exorcist
The Godfather
Holocaust (TV)
Jaws
Macbeth
Murder on the Orient Express
Nicholas and Alexandra
One Flew Over the Cuckoo's Nest
Picnic at Hanging Rock
Raid on Entebbe
Roots (TV)
Saturday Night Fever
Stalker
Star Wars
Tora! Tora! Tora!

INDEX